DISCUSSIONS OF WITTGENSTEIN

Discussions
of Wittgenstein

RUSH RHEES

SCHOCKEN BOOKS · NEW YORK

Published in U.S.A. in 1970
by Schocken Books Inc.
67 Park Avenue, New York, N.Y. 10016
© Rush Rhees 1970
Library of Congress Catalog Card No. 71–110251

Printed in Great Britain

CONTENTS

PREFACE

I am grateful to Professor G. P. Henderson for permission to reprint 'Miss Anscombe on the *Tractatus*' (*The Philosophical Quarterly*, Volume 10, January 1960); to the Editors of *The Philosophical Review* for 'The *Tractatus*: Seeds of Some Misunderstandings' (Volume LXXVII, April 1963) and for 'Some Developments in Wittgenstein's View of Ethics' (Volume LXXIV, January 1965); to Professor Peter Winch for ' "Ontology" and Identity in the *Tractatus*' from the volume *Studies in the Philosophy of Wittgenstein* (Routledge and Kegan Paul, 1969); to Professor S. Körner for 'The Philosophy of Wittgenstein' (*Ratio*, Volume VIII, December 1966); to Mr A. A. Kassman for 'Can there be a Private Language?' (*Aristotelian Society, Supplementary Volume XXVIII*, 1954), 'Wittgenstein's Builders' (*Proceedings of the Aristotelian Society*, 1959–60) and 'Unanswerable Questions' (*Aristotelian Society, Supplementary Volume XL*, 1966).

The essay 'On Continuity' has not been printed before and I wondered if I should include it. The ideas are Wittgenstein's, and so are the chief examples and phrases. The first half says little that cannot be found in Wittgenstein's own words in the *Remarks on the Foundations of Mathematics*. But it goes with the second half which discusses questions ('continuity outside mathematics') on which he did not write after 1930. I had been trying to write on continuity in 1938, and in August he offered to talk about it with me. For about three weeks we met every day. Once Francis Skinner was present; no one else was. The discussions were in the afternoon and they were long (one finished after seven hours). In the last few of them I took down some things while he was speaking. In the evenings or next day I wrote down what I had understood. I have written from these notes, trying at various points to work out what he meant.

The essay does not ask how the methods of representation in quantum theory may be related to conceptions of continuity in classical physics. None but a physicist could discuss this. Professor W. H. Watson has done so from a position in philosophy close to Wittgenstein's (*Understanding Physics Today*, Cambridge,

1963). The questions he raises are important, but they are not about 'puzzles in the idea of continuity', as Wittgenstein's are; and do not supersede them.

May 1969   RUSH RHEES

I

Miss Anscombe on the *Tractatus*

When students first read the *Tractatus* they are often impressed and feel that this is the sort of thing they had been hoping to find. But then, as often as not, they are baffled and feel they can make no headway. Miss Anscombe's book* is meant to help them to understand the most important topics. And if they can follow her in these, they will probably go on.

She says that most of what has been written about the *Tractatus* is wildly irrelevant. And probably she has often felt that she must make a point plain to those that have misunderstood it. She has had to take up a definite line of interpretation, and at certain points defend what she is doing. On the other hand, she has wanted to keep it a book for students and has felt that (as she puts it in one place) she must 'slur over' some of the difficulties 'for the purposes of a first rough exposition'. So that one is sometimes uncertain how to read it.

She seldom tries to paraphrase what Wittgenstein is saying. She wants to bring out what his questions are, and why he tries to answer them along the lines he does. She tries especially to show how his arguments have grown from the discussions of Russell and of Frege. These are often difficult, and if a student can follow her here, I wonder if he could not have followed more of her own criticisms. She wanted it to be a small book, and it would be hard to bring that in. She does mention some of the difficulties—the confusion between the meaning of a name and the bearer of a name, for instance. But she does not discuss the way in which this has influenced other things he says. If she had done that, she might have made plainer what Wittgenstein was trying to do.

* *An Introduction to Wittgenstein's Tractatus.* By G. E. M. Anscombe. (London: Hutchinson, 1959.)

She is best in what she says on special points or passages which have often been felt to be obscure. She has a particularly good account of Wittgenstein's treatment of 'A believes that p', for instance. But she is as good in what she says of sign and symbol, 'expressions', formal concepts and formal series, the general form of the proposition—and a number of other topics. My only question would be whether a student will see how her discussions of these different things hang together. He may wonder how they are related to any central theme. So that he still finds it hard to say what the *Tractatus* is really all about.

She makes 'the picture theory of the proposition' central for at least the first half of her book. But she does not show clearly how this is related to what Wittgenstein called 'the main point', in his letter to Russell from which she quotes in her last chapter. And with her account of the 'picture theory' I wonder if she could.

Wittgenstein said in that letter that 'my main contention, to which the whole business of logical propositions is only corollary . . . is the theory of what can be expressed (*gesagt*) by propositions—i.e. by language (and what comes to the same thing, what can be *thought*); and what cannot be expressed by propositions, but only shown (*gezeigt*); which I believe is the cardinal problem of philosophy . . .'. Everyone who reads the *Tractatus* knows that he does make this distinction. But why is it so important? In what way are the other discussions in the book only corollary to it? And why is it cardinal for logic?

In *Tractatus* 5.555 he asks, 'And anyway, how could I have been concerned in logic with forms that I can invent? Surely I must be concerned with what it is that enables me to invent them.' One reason why he was worried by the plurality of logical constants in *Principia* was that this made the development of the logical system seem arbitrary. Which would mean that there were forms of inference without any clear or necessary relation to one another; so that we might wonder at calling them all by the same name. If there were anything arbitrary about the introduction of a new form, then how could it be a *logical* form? This kind of difficulty might lead one to doubt the reality of logic, as truly as the logical paradoxes could. And there could be no point in constructing a logical system until it was met.

What makes it possible to develop logical formulae is what he calls the general form of operation. (Cf., e.g., 5.503.) Or we could say that it is the general form of proposition. And what he says about propositions in the earlier sections is important just because it leads up to these. Miss Anscombe shows that we cannot understand the general form of operation, or the general form of proposition, unless we have grasped what he says about formal concepts and formal series. Her discussion of this is perhaps the best thing in her book. And in what he says about formal concepts he is giving one of the most important examples of the distinction between what can be said and what can be shown. It is clear that he thinks we cannot understand either the reality of propositions or their connexion with logic except in this way.

He wanted to meet the difficulties not only of the logical paradoxes, but of anything suggesting that logic may be arbitrary. Anything which throws in question the difference between what is logic and what is not; anything which puts the *reality* of logic in question. Russell's theory of types was meant to meet doubts of this kind when they were born of the logical paradoxes. Wittgenstein did not think it could meet what he thought were the fundamental difficulties; for various reasons. And he was still less satisfied by the later developments which have spoken of a hierarchy of languages or of 'meta-languages'. These have mostly come since the *Tractatus*. But its distinction between what can be said and what can be shown is especially important for the kind of question they are discussing. For it is a rejection of any theory of 'foundations for logic' on the lines which certain writers have offered. Many of what Wittgenstein calls 'formal concepts' are what some would now call 'semantical concepts'. And we are told that one can 'establish' these concepts, and establish, for instance, the relation of propositions to reality, in terms of a meta-language. I do not think these writers have tried to meet what Wittgenstein does say about formal concepts. And Miss Anscombe's discussion of them should make this clear.

(In a remark written considerably later than the *Tractatus* Wittgenstein said 'No philosophical problem can be solved by a calculus.' He no longer spoke quite as he had in the *Tractatus*, but he always thought that 'meta-languages' were an evasion. This was not because he did not feel that logic was important, but because he was convinced that it was.)

There are difficulties about saying what a proposition is; and about any such statement as 'p is a proposition'. (If that is always empty, then what do you mean by talking about propositions at all?) There are difficulties for any account of what 'expressing a proposition' is; or in speaking of the relation of a sentence to what it says. Try explaining anything of the form '"p" says that p', for instance—which Wittgenstein says is also the form of 'A believes that p' or 'A thinks p'. In fact, the relation of a proposition to what it says, is the same as the relation of thought to what it thinks of. What the proposition says, or what I understand, is 'in' the proposition (even though in another sense it is independent of it), just as, when I think of this or that, it is in my thought. This is one reason for saying that a proposition is a picture of reality.

Wittgenstein's word for a picture—*Bild*—is connected with the verb *abbilden*. Miss Anscombe translates this by 'depicts', which is often misleading. And this may be one reason why she neglects what Wittgenstein calls the 'inner' similarity between picture and pictured. But there is nothing in English which quite covers it. And perhaps we should keep to the verb 'picture' and 'picturing', even if we have to use quotation marks. The idea of *Abbildung* came into logic from the mathematicians' practice of finding a model for one system in another: finding a model for a non-euclidean geometry in Euclid, for instance, or a model for geometry in the arithmetic of real numbers—which in German was called an *Abbildung* of the one system in the other. The method was used to show the consistency and validity of, say, Lobatchevsky's geometry. And I think Wittgenstein has it in mind when he speaks of the 'Logik der Abbildung' (in 4.015, for instance) and even when he speaks of an 'Abbildung der Wirklichkeit'. We have to translate this by 'picturing of reality', but we lose much of the connotation when we do; and in particular we lose the reference to a rule.

If we left out the idea of a general rule in connexion with picturing (and I think Miss Anscombe neglects it), we should nearly miss the point of the analogy. Why should anyone speak of a '*logical* picture', for instance? And what has logical form got to do with picturing? But what special importance has logical form in connexion with *saying* anything, for that matter? When Wittgenstein says that propositions are pictures of reality, one thing he wants to bring out is the way in which logic is fundamental in connexion with them.

4

It is the fact that there is a general rule by which we can derive them from one another which constitutes the inner similarity of the score and the music and the gramophone record—for all that these seem about as diverse as any things could be (4.0141). And he had just referred to this inner similarity when he said that the score and the music and the record 'stand to one another in that picturing internal relation (in jener abbildenden internen Beziehung zu einander) which holds between language and the world'. 'That there is a general rule—this is what it consists in.' This is what picturing consists in. So there must be a general rule of this sort whenever there is a proposition; whenever something is said.

At first sight the analogy sticks. The idea of a 'rule of projection' by which you can produce the music from the score, and derive the score from the music, is intelligible enough. We could speak of the score as an *Abbildung* of the music. Or again, of one language as an *Abbildung* of another. But what does it mean to say that 'language' is an *Abbildung* of *reality*? And what is 'picturing reality' anyway?

When Wittgenstein says (4.01) 'The proposition is a picture of reality', he adds: 'The proposition is a model of reality as we think it to be.' Now when we take one mathematical system as a model for another, we may examine the two systems independently. But not here; not when we are taking the proposition as a model of reality. It is easy to become confused about this because the *Tractatus* does say, for instance (4.05): 'Reality is compared with the proposition.' But this is when he is going on to discuss the difference between true and false propositions. And it is important not to confuse picturing reality with saying what is true. Not to confuse what we do when we want to decide whether a proposition is true or false, and what we do when we want to decide whether it has sense—i.e., whether it is a proposition at all. In the next sentence, after the one I just quoted, he says: 'It is only because it is a picture of reality that a proposition can be true *or* false' (4.06, my italics). And one might almost want to ask: 'Well, how do you know? How do you know there is any such picturing?'

You can understand a proposition—it is not just a jumble of words. But it is not just that the words have a definite arrangement, either. It is an arrangement which says something. And this difference, whatever it is, shows the proposition's relation

5

to reality. What we start with is just the recognition that it does say something. We do not start by recognizing any correlation between it and something else. And this makes it rather like recognizing something as a picture (not just a jumble of marks). We may say that we understand a picture, when we do not know the scene from which it is taken. Think of a 'still life', for instance; or a Dutch interior. It is a picture of what is in it. And we may see this without noticing its similarity to anything outside it.

Sometimes that is what we do notice, of course; it may be what interests us. I may be comparing a drawing of St Paul's with the church itself as I am looking at it. But I should see what the picture is, and in an important sense I should see what it is a picture of, even if I were not standing here and even if I had never heard of St Paul's. Only, then if you did ask me what it was a picture of, I should probably just point to the picture itself: 'See, it's this building, with an entrance here, and a dome here, etc.' And then what would it mean to speak of 'the relation of the picture to what it pictures'?

'Well, but we can *say* what is pictured. And, conversely, we can make a picture of what is said.' Does this amount to more than: We can say in one language what we can say also in another? Wittgenstein would agree that this does show something about reality and about language too. It does show something about 'saying something', if we show that you can sometimes draw it. But then the point is that the picturing is something they *both* do. Neither gets you any nearer than the other to 'what it really is'.

If I am performing an experiment I may write down a record or description of it as I go along. Could one say that my description is a copy of what I am describing? It is the experiment —what is happening here on the bench—that guides me in what I write, anyway. Yet if we say in Wittgenstein's sense that my sentences picture reality, this does not mean simply that they are a true description of what is happening. Rather it is because they do picture reality that they can describe anything at all. It is because of their logical form, because they are propositions, because they say something. Now suppose someone says: 'We could have made a film of the experiment, and this would have done as well. We could see in the film what happened.' Yes—if we can understand what we see. If you are a scientist yourself, then the film of the experiment may tell you as much as the scientist's own description. But as it stands, the film is extremely ambiguous—as the remark 'We can see in the film what happens' brings out.

So in what sense does the film picture the facts or picture reality? 'It is a photographic record of whatever was visible at the time'—but this hardly helps. If we do not know what those happenings were doing there—what the point or the significance of this and that was—then we shall hardly know what sense to make of the film. This is not simply a matter of being able to recognize what the various things in the film stand for. It is a matter of being able to recognize what kind of picture it is or how it hangs together.

When I describe the experiment, I am not just trying to do in a sketchy way what the film does completely. A proposition pictures, not because the signs in it have these physical features, but because of what they do. And it is the same with the film.

Wittgenstein even said (3.1431) that objects in space like tables and chairs and books might be symbols: that we could imagine a propositional sign composed of these instead of written signs; and their positions relative to one another would express the sense of the proposition. But here the point is that they do constitute a propositional sign. Each of them has a point which a written sign would have if we had been writing the proposition down. Their positions *vis-à-vis* one another have a point just as the order in which we write the signs has. Apart from this—apart from their recognizable roles in a propositional sign—they would not express anything at all.

It does not matter what we use as signs, if only we make clear the logical point of their combination. 'What is essential in a proposition is whatever it has in common with all propositions that can express the same sense' (3.341). If we say that 'The real name (der eigentliche Name) is that which all symbols which signify the same object have in common'—and Miss Anscombe shows the importance of this—we should also say that the real proposition is what is common to all the propositional signs which can express the same sense. And it is *this* which stands in the internal picturing relation with reality. This is why we may show something about reality if we show other ways of saying the same thing. For this brings out 'what the symbols have in common'. This is one reason why logical analysis is important, also.

7

We must emphasize this. 'What signifies, in any symbol, is what is common to all those symbols which, by the rules of logical syntax, may be substituted for it' (3.344). He goes on to say that what is common to all notations for truth functions is that they can be replaced by the notation of the Sheffer stroke. But the connexion between logical syntax and whatever is expressive in a proposition is important for all that we have been trying to say about picturing. We have spoken of recognizing it as a picture, or recognizing it as a proposition. Now suppose someone wondered whether there might be something arbitrary or personal in this. You just happen to find this group of signs intelligible—it says something to you—almost like a flower that arrests your attention; and this need have nothing to do with recognizing any other propositions at other times. Could it be like that? Wittgenstein would have said it could not. That would not have been recognizing a proposition at all. And to say that understanding a proposition might be something arbitrary in that way, would be self-contradictory.

You understand something that is said. It is possible to say something—i.e., there are expressions which picture reality. And a picturing of reality is possible because there is a general rule—a rule by which we distinguish between sense and non-sense.

There cannot be anything arbitrary in logic, because anything arbitrary would have to be *said*: and logic (the general rule) is what makes this possible.

Now part of the point here is that there must be logic if there are *empirical* propositions—propositions which we can understand without knowing whether they are true or false. Propositions which are either true or false, but whose truth or falsity depends on something external to them.

'If there would still be logic even if there were no world, then how could there be logic where there *is* a world?' (5.5521). As though the relation of logic to the world were external, in some way; so that what makes it *sensible* to talk of the possibility of anything's existing, would have nothing to do with logic. As though the truth or falsity of empirical statements, or the possibility of empirical statements at all, were something logic had nothing to do with. They would have to be 'independent of logic', then—and this is nonsense. (If only because you are using logical ideas when you call something independent of anything.) Miss Anscombe's elucidation of this is particularly helpful.

This is the importance of connecting logic with 'saying something' altogether. And of insisting that it is the logic of the language we speak, and not of some artificial or ideal language. And incidentally it helps to explain the idea of *Sprachlogik* or 'logic of language'.

A logic which was confined to formalized languages, for instance—or for which the distinction of true and false had sense only in formalized languages—would not be logic at all in the sense in which Wittgenstein is writing of it here. He used to say later that if there were a set of rules which we followed only in connexion with a particular game that we sometimes played, then we should hardly call them laws of thought—even if these were the only rules we had for 'and' and 'or' and 'not' and 'if . . . then'. We would call them laws of thought only if they went through the whole of our life.

We cannot deduce from anything *else* that they are applicable here. 'One thing is clear: The laws of logic cannot themselves be subject to further logical laws' (6.123). Any such suggestion would show a misunderstanding of the kind of laws they are, and of their relation to the propositions of which they hold.

This question of the relation of logic and empirical propositions has always been one of 'the cardinal problems of philosophy'. Most forms of scepticism have centred round it, for instance. But we cannot understand it unless we are clear about what can be said and what can only be shown. This is the point of the *Tractatus*.

There can be no *proving* that empirical propositions depend on logic—for what sort of 'dependence' would that be? Logic does not govern what can be said, in the sense of determining which of two contradictory propositions is to be asserted. 'Nothing can happen contrary to the laws of logic' would be meaningless; but so, of course, would 'everything happens *according* to the laws of logic'.

We recognize the relation of logic to empirical propositions when we see these propositions as picturing. This picturing can be made clearer by logical analysis; for in this we are bringing out what is common to all those propositions which express the same sense. We cannot *say* what is common to them. And what

9

the logical analysis shows—is just what ordinary propositions show. Only it is made clearer.

The analysis is given in a symbolism which avoids ambiguities of logical syntax—a symbolism which makes clear the ways in which the different signs signify. This brings out the sense of the proposition, or the way in which it pictures. But the sense has to be expressed in terms of truth and falsity, and we have to speak of 'picturing the existence and non-existence' of states of affairs. The logical constants make this possible, but they also make it easy to become mixed about the relation of a proposition to what it pictures.

The sense of a proposition must be independent of the facts. Yet we give the sense of a proposition when we give its 'truth conditions'—the conditions under which we should call it true, and the conditions under which we should call it false. So it may look as though the sense of a proposition just *is* its relation to the facts.

That the sense must be independent of the facts is something Wittgenstein emphasizes, for instance at 4.061. And he says that if we overlook this we are likely to think of 'true' and 'false' as two different relations that a sign may have to what it signifies—so that 'p' signifies truly what '~p' signifies falsely. But we understand a proposition when we understand what it *says*; and 'signifies' is misleading. When I say 'the iron is getting warmer', this may be true or false, but these are not two different ways of *saying* it. If it is false, it says just what it would if it were true. Otherwise I should never know *what* was true or false.

Or again: If a proposition makes sense, it must make sense to contradict it. If I am saying anything when I say the iron is getting warmer, then you will be saying something if you say it is not. But then we should not be saying the same thing in different ways. You would be saying the *opposite* of what I said.

It is the same proposition whether it is true or false. But it is not the same proposition as its negative. And, *nota bene*, it is the same proposition if it has the same sense. You cannot say 'If *it* had the opposite sense . . .'

When Wittgenstein says (4.0621) 'The propositions "p" and "~p" have opposite senses, but it is one and the same reality that corresponds to them', this means: one must have sense if the other does. And this is fundamental for the conception of 'having sense' altogether. It is one reason why he says that tautology and contradiction are not pictures of reality (4.462). But he is not using 'corresponds' in the way in which some people do when they speak of a true proposition as corresponding to the facts. What gives sense to 'p' is also what gives sense to '~p'. But what makes 'p' true is not what makes '~p' true.

And if 'p' is true—the truth is not a relation between the facts and what it says. I say the iron is getting warmer. If this is true, then what it says *is* a fact; not something else which corresponds to it.

I may say it when it is *not* a fact, of course. And this is the point of 'the sense is independent of the facts'.

What is the point in talking about picturing, unless it is to emphasize that you can say what is a fact and not something else which corresponds to it? The only 'something else' is the propositional *sign*—not the sense. And the sign is not what is said—it is not what may be true or false—it is what 'says'. It says what it does because it is the sign that it is. This is the 'picture theory'. And if the sign is the same, then it says the same—true or false.

At the start of her account of 'the picture theory' (p. 65) Miss Anscombe refers to Wittgenstein's remark: 'The proposition *shows* its sense. The proposition *shows* what is the case *if* it is true. And it *says that* it is the case.' And apparently this suggests to her that expressing a sense and saying it are different; so that a proposition might show what is the case while saying that it is not. (Or, as she would put it, 'show how things are while saying that they are not'.) But he says that a proposition shows its sense because, for instance, I can understand a sentence I have never heard before. I could not understand a *word* I had never met before, unless someone told me what it meant. But there is no 'meaning of the sentence' which I have to learn before I can understand it. It is not that kind of understanding. But it would be part of the same point if you said that no one can explain to me what *saying* something is. 'Saying' and 'having sense' are the same. And there is no difference between understanding the sense of a propositional sign and understanding what it says.

It is in *saying* something that a proposition pictures reality. In certain circumstances I may also *use* a picture in what I am saying. But this is irrelevant to the idea of a proposition itself as a picture.

On page 67 Miss Anscombe says: 'The picture theory of the proposition is that the proposition in the positive sense says: "This is how things are" and in the negative sense says: "This is how things aren't"—the *"this"* in both cases being the same: the comparison is a comparison with a picture of the "this" in question.' But if the 'this' is what the proposition says—and that is what it pictures—how can it be the same in both propositions? And can one speak of a proposition as saying anything *about* what it says? I should wonder then how it ever manages to say anything. What Miss Anscombe is calling a picture here seems more like a descriptive phrase, and not the proposition itself.

On page 70 she says that 'it is a peculiarity of a picture of something's being the case that it can be taken as presenting us with something that is the case by being a *picture of what is not the case*' (italics in text). In a footnote she explains that 'the problem is the ancient one of how a false proposition makes sense', and she refers to *Philosophical Investigations*, par. 429, where Wittgenstein says: 'The agreement, the harmony of thought and reality consists in this: if I say falsely that something is *red*, then, for all that, it is not *red*.' But she ought to have continued the quotation, which goes on: 'And that if I want to tell someone what "red" means in the sentence "That is not red", I do it by pointing to something red.' This does not mean that when I say falsely that the iron is red, there is any sort of agreement between what I say and the iron which is black; or that my false statement 'presents us' with that.

She then refers to Wittgenstein's early view that a proposition may be symbolized as having two poles, 'true' and 'false'. If I give the circumstances in which I call a proposition true, and also the circumstances in which I call it false, I have determined its sense. Or, in other words, 'the sense of the proposition is determined by the two poles, *true* and *false*'. And if we say that 'names are like points, propositions like arrows—they have sense' (*Tractatus* 3.144), I suppose we might think of the F pole at the arrow's tail, and the T pole at its head. But there is nothing in this to suggest that a proposition may have either of two different *senses*; quite the contrary. Yet Miss Anscombe says (p. 71): 'This rendering of the picture become proposition would stress the fact that it has acquired two "poles" or senses in which it can be thought.'

And on page 72 she has: 'Every picture-proposition has two

senses, in one of which it is a description of the existence, in the other of the non-existence, of a configuration of objects; and it is that by being a projection.' I think this should have shown her that there was something wrong. If that were Wittgenstein's view, he would be saying not only that a proposition has two senses, but that it has two *opposite* senses. And then it would be nothing you could believe or contradict or understand in any way at all.

If the sense is a configuration of objects, then it cannot be just the *spatial* configuration. It must have the complexity which we express with the logical constants. (Cf. 5.47: 'Where there is complexity, there is argument and function, and with these are all the logical constants.') This expression belongs to the picturing—to the kind of picture it is. And unless the picture is ambiguous, there are not two ways in which it can be taken.

Wittgenstein did hold that we may express the same proposition in an affirmative and in a negative way. Double negation shows this. We determine the sense of a proposition by giving both the conditions of its truth and the conditions of its falsity, and we can express the proposition by saying that it excludes the latter. We may call this taking the proposition in the negative sense. (And it is the same proposition, for 'if p implies q and q implies p, p and q are the same proposition'.)

This is the point of the passage (4.463) which Miss Anscombe quotes on page 64: 'The proposition, the picture, the model, are in a negative sense like a solid body that limits the freedom of movement of others; and in a positive sense like the space surrounded by a solid substance, in which a body is situated.' But she goes on to say: 'Here at any rate a proposition, as well as a picture or a model, is conceived as *something that can have both a positive and a negative sense*' (my italics). And this is a misunderstanding, or at least misleading.

There are positive and negative ways of *expressing* the same proposition. But they do not express different *senses* of the same proposition, for that means nothing. The double negation has the same sense as the proposition itself. On the other hand, the negative or contradictory of the proposition *does* have a different sense, and for this reason it is not a way of expressing the same proposition. (Unclarity here might make one mix up 'affirmative or negative' with 'true or false'.) But the *sense* is not negative in this case either. It is incompatible with what it contradicts; that is all.

In 4.023 Wittgenstein says: 'Die Wirklichkeit muß durch den Satz auf ja oder nein fixiert sein.' Miss Anscombe says (p. 17, footnote) she thinks 'we can see Wittgenstein's hand in the free but excellent rendering' of this as: 'The proposition determines reality to this extent, that one only needs to say "yes" or "no" to it to make it agree with reality.' But the passage goes on: 'And so reality must be described completely by it.' And if the translation of the first sentence is right, what is the connexion? Why the 'And so' ('Dazu')? And why *completely*?

Surely the point of the first sentence is what Wittgenstein puts when he speaks as though a proposition were dividing reality into the conditions of its truth and the conditions of its falsity; 'like a line', as he said in a slightly different connexion, 'which divides all points in a plane into right and left'.

In any case, you do not make it agree with reality by saying 'yes' or 'no' to it. If it agrees with reality at all, then it does not matter what you say.

I have been dwelling on a small part of what she says, because other things in her interpretation seem to turn on it. She is trying to guide us in accepting the picture theory for a time, so that we may follow the *Tractatus* more easily. And so she leaves the major difficulties, although she knows they are there. I cannot have said anything relevant that she has not recognized. But she thinks that this, with all its faults, is the view of the *Tractatus*; and I do not read it so.

The notebooks show that in the three or four years before the *Tractatus* was finished, Wittgenstein was changing his idea of 'picturing' in various ways, and that negative propositions gave him trouble. What he finally wrote in the *Tractatus* is in many things a long advance from those earlier remarks, even where they seem fairly similar. The conception of 'sense' is more carefully worked out; and so is the view of picturing in relation to logical form (including the general form of the proposition). Miss Anscombe has sometimes been guided by examples from the earlier notes, and has kept to features which, it seems to me, the *Tractatus* view excludes.

There are still difficulties in the view as he has it there, of course. 'Elementary propositions' and 'simple signs' cannot be made quite clear. And often when Miss Anscombe puzzles me, it is because she is trying to show how the 'edifice' depends on them. Much of the trouble about negation comes in this way. Most often, though, I have been helped, not puzzled, in reading her.

2

The *Tractatus*: Seeds of Some Misunderstandings

Professor Alexander Maslow wrote his essay, *A Study in Wittgen-stein's* Tractatus, in 1933. Twenty-eight years later he published it practically unchanged.* He says that many details of his exposition are 'derived from the lectures of and discussions with Professor Schlick' (to whom the book is dedicated) and that he has 'been generally strongly influenced by Schlick's logical positivism'.

In 1929 Wittgenstein discussed the idea of 'a phenomeno-logical language', and in connexion with this he spoke of 'hy-potheses' in the rather special way he did at that time; of these especially he would say that their sense was the method of their verification. During vacations from Cambridge he had regular discussions with Schlick and Waismann and some others. But Schlick and the logical positivists never followed him closely, although they borrowed a good deal. When Maslow is making the original contributions of his first two chapters he uses, or misuses, many of Wittgenstein's examples without acknowledg-ment. For example, he thinks that the *Tractatus* makes the grammar of colour words depend on physical laws, and he says that 'to illustrate [the metaphysical character of this] we might use a simile. Let us imagine rigid bodies, say cubes, made of some invisible material, say solidified air, and each painted on only one face. . . . Let us assume that we are restricted to visual experiences; we shall then be able to experience only the coloured squares but not the other parts of the cubes. Let us as-sume that we can move the coloured squares about. We will find that we cannot move the coloured squares entirely arbitrarily; this is so of course because the invisible cubes of which the squares are faces prevent certain movements. From the ex-

* Berkeley and Los Angeles: University of California Press, 1961.

perience of moving these squares, we may derive a law for the motion of coloured squares, which may lead to a postulate that there are invisible cubes attached to each of our squares and that our laws of the possible relations of coloured squares in space are due to the properties of the invisible squares' (p. 34).

Now in February 1931 Wittgenstein had written in his note-book: 'Suppose we had perfectly transparent glass cubes, each with one side coloured red. When we bring them together, we find that only certain spatial arrangements are possible, be-cause of the cubic form of the bodies. I might then give the rule of the ways in which such red squares can be ordered without ever mentioning the cubes; but the property of the cubic form would be there in the rule nevertheless. Not, of course, that they are glass cubes, but the geometry of the cube.'

When Wittgenstein wrote this he had been discussing the meaning of negation, and also of 'is'. He had been interested in the fact that there are different meanings of negation, besides those which appear in the truth-functional calculus. And he was interested in the question of what it is when the same word is understood in different senses. He had just been asking, in this passage, 'What kind of proposition is it if I say: "The word 'is' in 'The rose is red' is the same as in 'The book is red', but not the same as in '2 × 2 is 4' "?' He goes on, 'I want to make this comparison: that the word "is" has a different verbal body [*Wortkörper*] behind it in the one case and in the other. That in each case it is the same surface, but belonging to a different body; as when I see a triangle in the foreground which is now the end surface of a prism and now of a tetrahedron.' After he has given the simile of the glass cubes and the geometry of the cube, he asks: 'But how can a cube, or the drawing (which amounts to the same thing here), serve as a notation for geo-metrical rules? Only by being a proposition belonging to a sys-tem of propositions: a cube with a red end surface will signify something different from a pyramid with a square red base, and so on. In other words, it will signify that property of the rules by which a cube is distinguished from a pyramid.'

This idea of a 'word body' (more often he used the term *Bedeutungskörper* or 'meaning body') was analogous to an earlier idea of a '*Beweiskörper*' or body of a proof. A year or more earlier he had written, 'We might also say: a completely analysed proposition in mathematics is its own proof. Or again:

a mathematical proposition is just the immediately visible surface of the whole body of proof [*des ganzen Beweiskörpers*], the boundary or side facing us.' Neither in this case nor in the other could the simile well express the dependence of anything on natural laws.

Wittgenstein came to distrust speaking or writing of *Bedeutungskörper*, for he thought it opened the way to 'mythology'. It was meant to represent the different 'facets' of the grammars of words, which he now saw to be complicated in ways not allowed for in the *Tractatus*. In 1929 he had come to see that the truth-functional calculus gives only a *part* of the grammar of 'and', 'or', 'not', and 'if . . . then'. They are used in ways which cannot be reduced to their use in logic—although such uses are not cut off from their use in logic, either.

One consideration among the many which helped him to see this was the difficulty Maslow mentions: that we cannot say both that this spot is now red and also that it is green. Maslow misunderstands the *Tractatus* on this (6.3751), but he sees that it affects the whole logical position.

When he wrote the *Tractatus* Wittgenstein thought that 'The spot is not green' could follow from 'The spot is red' only if the affirmative proposition ('The spot is red') were the logical product of the denial (not green) and some other proposition. But he had not worked this out. The *Tractatus* says clearly that colour propositions like 'This is red' and 'This is green' are not elementary propositions and that their conjunction is logically impossible. But since the structures were left obscure, perhaps it was natural for some to assume, as Maslow does, that Wittgenstein was thinking of the structures of the physical counterparts—the light waves. (Even in the early passage in the *Notebooks*—page 81—Wittgenstein says clearly that it is not a physical impossibility but a logical one. The impossibility of a motion's having two velocities at once is a logical impossibility, too, as is also the impossibility of two bodies in the same place.)

How should we express the incompatibility of the colours? When Wittgenstein was working on this in 1929 it seemed to him at first that we describe the colour of the spot by specifying the various shades we see in it, adding that these are *all* the shades, since we can see that while the spot is this colour it cannot have any other colour.

But if 'These are all' is a proposition, then the enumeration of the various shades without that ending must be a proposition, too: one which, although it ascribes a colour to something, does not thereby exclude any other colour.

Again, what about the compatibilities of the elementary colours or shades themselves? We sometimes say that this colour has more red in it than that. If this means there are different amounts of red, they are incompatible with one another. And how should this incompatibility be expressed?*

> *ag* and *ar* contradict one another although—or rather because—each has sense by itself. And if we keep the meaning of '·' then we cannot write the conjunction of them; or else the propositions themselves have different meanings when we do.
>
> And what of the disjunction? '*a* is either green or red' is clearly not nonsense. But if $p \lor q$ is not nonsense, then $p \cdot q$ is not nonsense, either.
>
> So apparently 'and' has a different meaning here from '·' in logic and analogously for disjunction.

Wittgenstein discussed this in his paper in the Aristotelian Society Supplementary Volume of 1929. Maslow refers to this paper more than once, but he does not say anything of its bearing on the remarks in *Tractatus* 6.3751. He rightly says that the 1929 view 'would have to be followed by a serious modification, if not a complete abandonment, of Wittgenstein's theory of molecular propositions as truth functions of logically independent atomic propositions, and of his theory of inference'. Maslow wants to avoid this by refusing to treat such colour propositions as elementary. (I think the new translation is right in preferring 'elementary' to 'atomic'.) He does not suggest how any analysis of them could prevent the reappearance of the difficulty. But whether they are elementary or not, the difficulty, or the greater part of it, remains.

One consequence was that Wittgenstein spoke more of 'grammar', as in 'the grammar of colour'. To speak of the logical syntax of colour would be confusing for the reasons just mentioned. But we could give an analysis of colour propositions

---

* Cf. Wittgenstein's *Philosophische Bemerkungen*, Oxford, 1964, pp. 106–11.

by exhibiting their grammar, or exhibiting the grammar of colour. In order to say what various colours are, we have to give their relations to other colours—as in the colour octohedron, for instance. This is a spatial representation and it can be misleading. We are concerned with 'internal' relations of colours; and although these show an analogy with a spatial order, this is not complete. A shade of orange is between red and yellow, but 'between' does not mean just what it does when we speak of a position between two others. We cannot ask what shade is exactly midway between pure red and pure yellow, for instance. We cannot say that colour intervals are divisible in just the ways that intervals in visual space are divisible. And so on. We need to understand the sense of 'more' and 'less' in speaking of colours. All this would belong to their analysis, but this is not the analysis which went with the calculus of truth-functions. So it would mean nothing to ask whether colour statements are elementary propositions or not.

When he was discussing the incompatibilities of colour statements, Wittgenstein wanted 'a purely phenomenological theory of colour' which would include nothing 'hypothetical' like references to light waves or to the physiology of the retina: colours as they are given in 'immediate experience'. And he suggested that we might have a 'phenomenological language' which would take in also the phenomena of visual space, of sounds, and so on: 'an account free of everything hypothetical' —which meant not only references to physics or physiology, but also any reference to the future or the past. ('That looks like a thunder storm coming up' is a hypothesis awaiting future verification. 'That looks grey' has nothing hypothetical.)

The notion of 'immediate experience' went with this special sense of 'description', in which we may speak of describing how it appears, or of describing a sense datum. Sometimes he seemed to be suggesting that the phenomena or sense data themselves might function as signs which were by nature symbols. But he saw that this would be a mistake. Apart from other and obvious difficulties, it would suggest that there was one form of expression which was nearer to reality than any other can be: something to which all less direct ways of speaking could be reduced. But this notion of 'reduction' would be a confused one. We may translate from one language to another or from one notation to another, but it would make no sense to say that this brought us nearer to the true way of expressing things. It is important to emphasize this, because he later saw that there is something of the same mistake in the *Tractatus*.

We cannot do without signs; but neither can we do without 'hypotheses'. Wittgenstein remarked once that a description which had nothing hypothetical—no sort of reference to anything past or future, for instance—would never interest anyone. He saw that expressions of immediate experience—he sometimes called them 'propositions in the strict sense'—have no sense or reality in themselves. They are significant only in their connexions with hypotheses, as the points at which hypotheses are verified.

An important difference between the propositions of immediate experience and elementary propositions, then, is that the propositions of immediate experience are not 'self-contained'. This has appeared already in their compatibilities and incompatibilities with one another, as shown in their special grammars. But their connexions with hypotheses are no less essential and no less important. They give sense to hypotheses: without them hypotheses would have no possible connexion with reality. But they have their own sense in hypotheses—as 'sections' through hypotheses. There is a logical connexion here, but it is not that of elementary propositions and truth functions. Truth functions depend on elementary propositions for their sense, but not in the way in which hypotheses depend on immediate experience.

Wittgenstein gave up the idea of a phenomenological language (a few months after he had suggested it), but for a time he spoke of 'phenomenology' as concerned with the grammars or the *possibilities* of the various sensory fields. Possible: what can be thought or what makes sense. Of course it has nothing to do with what is psychologically possible, though this is how Maslow takes it (pp. 35, 36). It does not make sense to *ask* if I can imagine a tone in unison with its third, or a red spot that is green. And to this extent immediate experience still seemed to show the reality of thought or the reality of language: what it is for language to have sense, what it is for there to be language at all.

This is also what the *Tractatus* was meant to show. And it is in this that elementary propositions are fundamental. 'All propositions are truth functions of elementary propositions.' We might say other things about them or about language; but it is in this that they show their sense, or show that they form a language. If we ask whether there are elementary propositions, we shall be asking whether there is any relation of thought to reality, or any reality in thought or in language.

This cannot mean 'whether there *sometimes* is a relation of thought and reality', as though it were one that is found to 'hold', as a causal relation may be. If, in the *Tractatus*, there is a general rule for the analysis of propositions, this is because there is a general rule for what thinking is: a general distinction between sense and nonsense, a conception of what can be said or what can be thought. If we say that the relation of thought and reality is not arbitrary, we are saying that what can be thought —or the distinction between what can be thought and what cannot—is not arbitrary.

So if we say that there are elementary propositions, this is not an arbitrary assumption. There can be no general criteria for identifying them, except the formal one that an elementary proposition is not a truth function of any further proposition, and the 'internal' one that an elementary proposition shows its sense immediately. There is no general account of the *subject matter* of elementary propositions, no general account of what the elements of thinking are, nothing to tell us what is the ultimate furniture of the world.

They show their sense immediately. I think Maslow misses this; perhaps he would say it was psychological. He misquotes *Tractatus* 5.1363 which concerns self-evidence and belief in the truth of a proposition. But elementary propositions are not self-evident, and it is not a question of their truth; just that they say something.

3

'Ontology' and Identity in the *Tractatus* à propos of Black's *Companion*

If we ask what Wittgenstein means by 'adequate symbolism', we shall look to the relation of sign and syntax; for it depends on that. So it is pointless to say, as Black does: we must have some view of what reality is like, before we can ask if the symbolism is adequate to describe it. Black takes this as a reason for his remarks about 'the ontology of the *Tractatus*'. For instance: 'Wittgenstein expects a perspicuous *view* of the nature of logic to have *ontological implications*.' 'Wittgenstein's conception of the nature of language . . . *required a stand on ontological issues*.' 'His ontology [*sic*] *is on the whole suggested by* his views about language.'* (My italics throughout.) This is confused, and the remarks about adequate symbolism in the *Tractatus* do not need it.

Since there are signs, there must be a distinction of true and false propositions—a distinction to be decided finally by observation, not by logic. We could say that the *truth* of logical principles is tied to this. When the *Tractatus* says in 6.113 that 'What distinguishes logical propositions is that we can see by the symbol alone that they are true', it adds: 'So what is especially important is the fact that the truth or falsity of non-logical propositions *cannot* be seen in the proposition alone.'—In other words, it would have no sense at all to speak of logical propositions unless there were empiricial propositions.

Mathematics is not written in tautologies, it is written in equations. But equations would be meaningless unless there were calculation: they get their reality from the general form of logical operation, and so from the internal relations of

* Max Black, *A Companion to Wittgenstein's* Tractatus, Cambridge, 1964, pp. 4, 7, 8.

propositional forms. So we could not treat mathematics as a logical method—we could not see that mathematical proofs are logical proofs—unless *empirical* statements had sense and could be the bases of logical operations.

This is summed up in 4.0312, which expresses the 'Grund-gedanke' of the book:

> Die Möglichkeit des Satzes beruht auf dem Prinzip der Vertretung von Gegenständen durch Zeichen.
> Mein Grundgedanke ist, daß die 'logischen Konstanten' nicht vertreten. Daß sich die *Logik* der Tatsachen nicht vertreten läßt.

This is at the foundation of what Wittgenstein has to say about logical analysis—e.g. (in 4.221) 'that in the analysis of propositions we must arrive at elementary propositions, consisting of names directly connected to one another'. He is contrasting this 'unmittelbare Verbindung' of names in elementary propositions with whatever it is that logical constants express. For these appear only in the expression of the results of an operation *on* elementary propositions. You can always transform a proposition containing logical constants into another equivalent to it. But elementary propositions cannot be equivalent to one another.—We can carry out logical operations independently of the truth or the falsity of elementary propositions: independently of what is the case. We can do this *because* of the fundamental difference between elementary propositions and others: i.e., because the logical constants 'do not stand for anything'. Otherwise we could not 'see by the symbol alone' that a calculation or a formal proof was correct.

The *Tractatus* could not begin with a discussion of logical constants and the truth of logical principles. What comes first is the truth or falsity of *material* propositions—in other words *sense*. Without this we could not even speak of *possible* signs.

But to call this 'ontology' is confusing. And to say that the discussions of logic are important because of the ontology which is built on them, is to stand the whole thing on its head. Black quotes the remark in Wittgenstein's 1913 *Notes on Logic*: '[Philosophy] consists of logic and metaphysics, the former its basis', and Black adds: 'Logic as the *basis* of metaphysics: throughout the book Wittgenstein expects a perspicuous view of the nature of logic to have ontological implications. Logic is important because it leads to metaphysics' (*Companion*, p. 4). But the remark he quotes does not say that logic is the basis of metaphysics; it says it is the basis of *philosophy*. And Wittgenstein did not say there or anywhere else that logic has *implications*.

Sentences like 'Der Name bedeutet den Gegenstand' (3.203) or 'Der Name vertritt im Satz den Gegenstand' (3.22) belong to the grammar of the words 'name' and 'object' and 'proposition'. The *Notes Dictated to Moore* had said (*Notebooks*, pp. 109, 110): 'In the expression (∃y) . φy, one is apt to say this means "There is a *thing* such that . . .". But in fact we should say "There is a y, such that . . ."; the fact that y symbolizes expressing what we mean. . . . In our language names are *not things*: we don't know what they are: all we know is that they are of a different type from relations, etc., etc.' The *Tractatus* might not put it in just this way, but the main point holds there.

'TOKEN OR TYPE?'

In connexion with 3.203—'A name means an object. The object is its meaning. ("A" is the same sign as "A".)'—Black asks 'Is the propositional sign a token or a type?'; and he goes on: 'When we normally speak of a sentence, we use the word "sentence" in a "type-sense" rather than a "token-sense". . . . That this is the way Wittgenstein himself uses the expression "propositional sign" (which takes over the role of "sentence" in his conception) is made quite clear by his remark at 3.203: " 'A' is the same sign as 'A'." If two propositional signs consist of physically similar words respectively attached to the *same* bearers, Wittgenstein counts the two as instances of the same propositional sign.'

But Wittgenstein himself said nothing of the sort: the text says nothing at all about physically similar signs respectively attached to the same bearers.

His remark in the *Notes Dictated to Moore* that 'in our language names are *not things*' says something about the grammar of 'name' and 'thing'; or as he puts it there, the difference in *logical type*. So, for instance, 'identity' has different rules of syntax when we speak of the identity of a thing and when we speak of the identity of a sign. ' "A" is the same sign as "A" ' expresses—or 'seeks to express'—the identity of a sign. It does not say anything. And it cannot be analysed in terms of 'this scratch here resembles that scratch there'. Perhaps we'd never say 'it's the same sign' unless the scratches did resemble one another, but this is not part of what we *mean* by ' "A" is the same sign as "A" '.—'How do you know this is A?' would be as nonsensical as 'How do you know this is white?'

A mark without syntax is not a sign. And this makes it hard to say what the identity of a sign is.

When Peirce* and others write about Types and Tokens they seem to feel that we might analyse the identity of a sign in terms of the identity of a physical object or of an event. But they never manage to: this is plain when Peirce calls a Token an '*instance*' of a Type, and when Ramsey says that '*a proposition* is a type whose instances consist of all propositional sign tokens which have in common, not a certain appearance, but a certain *sense*'. The 'all'—in 'all propositional sign tokens which . . .'—is bewildering, but since each of these has a sense, it ought to refer to various propositions which are *equivalent* to one another; and if we put it so, we are back where we started: distinguishing type and token has done nothing.—On the other hand, physical similarity between particular scratches cannot be what 'groups tokens together into types', in Peirce's sense of Type; no more than grouping shells or pebbles together would be treating them as Tokens.

Black thinks Wittgenstein uses 'propositional sign' for a *class* of *token* propositional signs. But what does 'token' add here?

When a printer estimates the number of words on a page he is speaking of physical marks, and it does not matter whether they are really words or not. Peirce calls the Token in which a Type is embodied 'an *Instance* of the Type'. But then if I count the instances of various Types on a page I am not counting what the printer counts.

'You cannot make the same scratch twice' could have sense. 'You cannot write the same word twice' could not.

'How can I be sure I am seeing the same token and not a different one? Maybe I am not reading the same copy of the book although I thought I was. Maybe someone had erased that word on that line and printed it again. Etc., etc.' Peirce might have answered, 'All right, you probably can't; and in such cases *it does not matter*.'—I.e., 'Tokens' always means 'Tokens on this page' or '. . . in this copy of this book'—or something of this sort. It is *not* a term for a kind of physical ob-

* C. S. Peirce, *Collected Papers*, Vol. IV, §§4.537, 4.538, 4.544.

ject, like 'scratch'. Ramsey and Black (and Peirce) are not clear about the grammar of it.

If nobody ever said anything, nothing would ever be said. And every time you write a word, you write a word.

But this is just as trivial as it sounds. It does not explain the meaning of 'That's a word'.

If I said 'They are all instances of "word"', you would probably take me to mean: 'We'd call them all words.' But of course this does not mean 'They are all Tokens of the Type "word"' in Peirce's sense.

We want to know the syntax of 'sign'. And we think, perhaps, that then we'd know the syntax of *signs*—i.e., what they must have in order to be signs.

Is it not the syntax of words that determines the syntax of 'word'? Unless you *understood* words in their syntax, you would not know what a word is, and you could not use the word 'word'. —If we say this, we do not mean—we *deny*—that the syntax of 'word' is given (or determined) by instances of the Type 'word'.

Black lands in this confusion because he thinks there *is* something by which our grammar is determined—or that this is how the *Tractatus* must be read. This goes with what he says about ontology in his discussion of 'adequate symbolism'.

'THE NAMING RELATION'

We speak in a different sense (1) of a proposition corresponding with reality (this is *Abbildung* or 'projection') and (2) of a name corresponding to what it means or to what is called by it.

When the *Tractatus* says, in 3.3: 'it is only in the connexion of a proposition that a name has meaning', it means that without the picturing or projection in a proposition there would be no correspondence at all. A proposition can describe a state of affairs in a language. Apart from a language it would not be a proposition. In *Tractatus* 5: 'A proposition is a truth function of elementary propositions.' So the combination of signs in a proposition is not arbitrary.* I am committed to the signs I use and the ways I combine them—by the general rule, the syntax

---

* Cf. 5.47: '... Wo Zusammengesetztheit ist, da ist Argument und Funktion, und wo diese sind, sind bereits alle logischen Konstanten.' Or 4.0141: 'Daß es eine allgemeine Regel gibt ... darin besteht eben die innere Ähnlichkeit dieser scheinbar so ganz verschiedenen Gebilde. Und jene Regel ist das Gesetz der Projektion. ...'

of the language. It is through this that the marks and sounds become symbols.

'There might have been a *different* correlation (of signs and things).' Alternatives are possible in a language. But a jumble of sounds or scratches would not be an alternative; it would mean nothing to call it one.

'But assigning names is arbitrary—*definitions* are arbitrary.'— What makes it a definition? If I give a name to a colour or a shape, I must have distinguished these as I distinguish expressions of a language. And within the language my definition commits me in certain ways, not in others. What the definition establishes—the relation of the name to what it stands for—is not an external relation.

We could say that the rules of multiplication are fixed by definition; in certain algebras these rules mean nothing. Or we might say that 4 is the result of 2 × 2 by definition; and this would not make the relation of result and multiplication a contingent one.—Words are related to what they say as a result to its calculation.

The *Tractatus* hardly distinguishes naming and calling something by its name. And 3.3 shows that this is not an oversight. 'Nur im Zusammenhange des Satzes hat ein Name Bedeutung.' So we may think that what the word 'red' means is expressed by the sentence 'a is red'.

Someone might say: 'The name must correspond to some reality. It cannot describe anything if there is nothing which it signifies.' Or suppose I told you: 'I call each of these roses red because each of them *is* red. The word I use corresponds to the colour of the flower.'—But what corresponds is the *sentence*. The *Tractatus* supposed that 'red' determines how I use it.

Wittgenstein rejected this later. It confuses giving a sample and using a sample. I may give a sample—a piece of coloured paper—to explain what I mean by 'vermilion'. Or I may use the sample in place of the word and tell you 'the flowers in that bed are *this* colour'. But I cannot use the sample to explain what colour this *sample* is.

The idea had been that the sample can serve as a 'primary sign'—one which explains itself and cannot be misunderstood. Other signs may be explained by the primary signs; but without the primary signs we'd never know what we were saying. Wittgenstein brought out the confusions in all this. But it showed that the distinction between what a name means and what is called by it is not always simple or easy.

Black knows that the meaning and the bearer of a name are different. But in his remarks on 'difficulties about the naming relation' he seems to think that *arbitrary* means *contingent* and that this means *empirical*. On page 116 he says: 'It is only *contingently* the case that the elements of [the propositional sign] F have the bearers that are attached to them, *since it is perfectly conceivable that F might have had a different sense.*' I have put the last clause in italics, for this does *not* show that: 'F says (so and so)' is an empirical proposition.

If the meanings of names are arbitrarily fixed, this does not mean that the sense of a *sentence* is arbitrarily fixed. What fixes the meaning of a name is a rule. But if someone says 'an arbitrary rule is a contingent proposition', he confuses a rule with a generalization.

IDENTITY

What shows that a name now means what it meant then? What shows that this statement speaks of the same thing as that?

4.243: 'Can we understand two names without understanding whether they signify the same thing or two different things?— Can we understand a proposition in which two names occur without knowing whether their meaning is the same or different? ...'

5.53: 'That what is meant is the same I express by using the same sign, and not by using a sign for identity. [und nicht mit Hilfe eines Gleichheitszeichens.] ...'

Wittgenstein does not ask 'What shows that this is the same sign?'—nor *can* this be asked. Yet Black seems to think the *Tractatus* tries to answer it. He sees that in 5.53–5.534 Wittgenstein wants 'to show that identities are not truth functions of elementary propositions, as genuine propositions are' (*Companion*, p. 290), but then he says: 'The basic idea is to show identity of objects, whether identified by names or included in the ranges of given variables, *by means of physical similarities* in the signs for such names and such variables.' I have put that phrase in italics.

Wittgenstein's point is that identity is not a function, not a tautology and not a logical principle; also that there is no 'general concept of logical identity' (compare e.g. Tarski's *Introduction*, p. 61).

Wittgenstein could call the laws of logic—the modus ponens, say, or double negation—propositions about propositions. The *Tractatus* brings out this relation of tautologies to genuine propositions by writing them both as truth functions. But x = y, or x = x, is not a truth function. This is the main point. The details of *Principia Mathematica*'s definition—'x and y are called identical when every predicative function satisfied by x is also satisfied by y'—are less important.

Principia Mathematica distinguished the '=' of definition from the '=' in x = y but assumed that here (in x = y) it is the same as the sign of equality in mathematics. Wittgenstein called this a confusion.

To arrive at cardinal numbers *Principia Mathematica* treats of Unit Classes and of Cardinal Couples; and so (e.g., *51.232) of 'the class whose only members are x and y'. To express this: if any third term, z, be assumed to belong to the given class, then z = x . v . z = y; and *PM* treats this formula as a function. A little later it says, 'the class of all couples of the form $\iota'x \cup \iota'y$ (where x ≠ y) is the cardinal number 2'—where the sign in the parenthesis does not express mathematical inequality. *Couples*, apparently, are entities correlated in the form x = a . y = b . v . x = c . y = d . v . . . . etc. Here the sign of identity would be used to express logical correlation but not mathematical equality.

For '*only* x and y have a given property' the *Tractatus* gives a notation in 5.5321:

$$(\exists x, y) . \varphi x . \varphi y : \sim(\exists x, y, z) . \varphi x . \varphi y . \varphi z.$$

The *Tractatus* does not introduce numbers in this way. But it shows that what *Principia Mathematica* wants to express can be written without the ambiguous z = x.v.z = y. Here it seems to be using the *PM* symbolism. But the apparent variables are different signs from those which *Principia Mathematica* writes the same way; for there the apparent variables seem to have the generality of a concept. The criticism of identity is also a criticism of the *Principia Mathematica* use of quantifiers—which the *Tractatus* has just been discussing.

It seems as if *Principia Mathematica* explains what it is we say about x and y when we call them identical. Just as it seems to say of those things which form a couple that they stand in this (which?) relation to one another. Perhaps Russell thought that unless he did treat x = y as a function he could not write the propositions of arithmetic in logical notation.

Ramsey seemed to accept the criticism of Russell's *definition* of identity. But he wanted to keep x = y as a function; so it looks at first as though he had kept the substance of Russell's theory. 'x = y is a function in extension of two variables. Its value is tautology when x and y have the same value, contradiction when x, y have different values'.* But these are not functions in Russell's or Frege's sense; so that when Ramsey speaks of 'an apparent variable φ_e', for instance, we do not know what he is saying. What he did share with Russell was a confusion about the application of mathematics and the reference to *things*.

He said (p. 49) that 'Wittgenstein's convention (regarding identity) . . . puts us in a hopeless position as regards classes, because . . . we can no longer use x = y as a propositional function in defining classes. So the only classes with which we are now able to deal are those defined by predicative functions. . . . Mathematics then becomes hopeless because we cannot be sure that there is any class defined by a predicative function whose number is two; for things may all fall into triads which agree in every respect, in which case there would be in our system no unit classes and no two-member classes.'

Apparently Ramsey rejects the formulations of *Tractatus* 5.321 on the ground that any such proposition might be false— we cannot be sure that the facts would justify it: 'things may all fall into triads'. And the advantage of (Ramsey's) functions in extension would be that the correlation here is arbitrary: the assertion of such functions does not depend on whether individuals agree or disagree in their properties.

Wittgenstein would say then as he said later: 'The application of mathematics in our language does not say what is true and what is false, but what is sense and what is nonsense.'

ARITHMETIC

Ramsey and Russell wanted to express arithmetic—mathematics—in logical terms: in terms of relations between functions. The *Tractatus* holds that the propositions of mathematics are equations and that these show *the logic of the world* as tautologies

* F. P. Ramsey, *The Foundations of Mathematics*, p. 53.

do: but they are not tautologies. ('The logic of the world'— roughly, we speak in the same way of *necessity* and of *impossibility* here as in logic.)

Russell's notation for numerical expressions does not show their internal connexion with operations such as addition and multiplication. The *Tractatus* holds that we understand numbers when we see them as features of a formal system or a calculation. 'Die Zahlen treten mit dem Kalkül in die Logik ein.'* A correlation between signs on one side and the other of an implication will not provide this; no more than it gives a conception of formal series.—Suppose we showed that it is the expression of an identity. What is there mathematical about this? How does the conception of '. . . and so on' come into it? How is it the expression of a *rule*?

This is a criticism of Russell's view of the *generality* of mathematics and of logic.

Suppose we said that the result of a calculation holds universally. This is of the same form as saying that the development of a given decimal is periodic. It is what Wittgenstein in the *Tractatus* expressed by 'the general term of a formal series' or 'the general form of number'. And, as he remarked later, the 'generality' of [1, x, x+1] cannot be expressed by '(x) . [1, x, x+1]'. (He was speaking of induction and the idea of 'holding for all numbers'.)

We might feel like saying that the general form of operation was the same as the general concept of a formal series—except that there is not really any such concept; it is a form. And we need to keep this distinction especially when we are speaking of generality. The *sign* for an operation is the general sign for a member of a formal series. Take that given in 5.2522: [a, x, O'x]. This is also the general form of *successive application* of an operation. For the general form of operation *is* the general form of its successive application. But it would be misleading to say that this shows 'the kind of generality which an operation has'. We might distinguish more general and more special operations, but this would be something else. It would not be the generality of the *form* (as opposed, say, to the generality of a concept).

'Numbers are exponents of operations.' They are not properties of aggregates, nor properties of the defining properties of aggregates. To say 'the successive applications of an operation

* *Philosophische Bemerkungen*, p. 129.

form an aggregate' would be nonsense. It would be treating 'repetitions of the operation' as physical events. It would confuse the form, or the possibility, with *my carrying out* the operation. This would be like a confusion of counting in mathematics —counting the roots of an equation or the inner and the outer vertices of a pentagram (Wittgenstein's examples)—and counting outside mathematics: counting the jars on a shelf or the white corpuscles in a blood sample.

We may want to say 'The order of successive application is a *temporal* order: one after another.' This is all right if we remember that it is an order of possibilities—the order in a construction. 'We cannot construct the polygon before the triangle' (Simone Weil). This does not refer to the times of actual happenings.

One reason for speaking of numbers as exponents of an operation was to show that the expressions of arithmetic belong to a system. Otherwise equations would be arbitrary rules of substitution. We should not know where they belonged; i.e., we should not know what to do with them. Black seems confused about this when he speaks of 'the applications of arithmetic to counting' (p. 314).

He is more seriously confused in what he says of 6.02. Here (p. 314) Black seems to take the successive application of an operation (his phrase 'the self-application of an Ω-operation' is not in the *Tractatus* and is misleading) to be something like the logical addition of a truth function to itself. p v p = p; so if the operation were 'v' ,then O'O'O'a would be the same as O'a. (Cf. 5.2521.) Black may have been led to this by the fact that when Wittgenstein begins his definitions or rather constructions of numbers he decides that the sign for the repetition of the same operation shall be an exponent written first as a succession of '+1's'. But this is the '+' of *arithmetical* addition. Whatever difficulties it may carry here, it is not logical addition.

$$p \vee p = p$$
$$1 + 1 \neq 1$$

As the *Tractatus* uses 'operation', it would be nonsense to speak of a logical sum of operations. And although throughout its successive application the operation is the same, this does not mean that the successive application is no different from a single application of it.

Black concludes: 'It would seem that for all m and n greater than zero, we must have $\Omega^m x = \Omega^n x$. Does it follow that m = n for all positive integers?'—But what does '=' mean in the first of these sentences? If it means 'is the same operation as', then nothing follows about arithmetical equality. If it is the sign of numerical equality, then I have no idea what the whole expression means. (Black's 'for all m and n greater than zero, we must have . . .' is nonsense in this context.)

In 6.01 Wittgenstein had said that the general form of operation is 'the most general form of transition from one proposition to another'. The result of any transition of this form would be a proposition, not a number. The general form of operation does enter somehow into the formal series in which numbers are generated, apparently. But the first idea is that numbers are *exponents* of the successive application of an operation—not that they are generated by it. The formal series in which they *are* generated or constructed is a series of *arithmetical* operations.

In 5.2523 the *Tractatus* says: 'Der Begriff der successiven Anwendung der Operation ist äquivalent mit dem Begriff "und so weiter".'—The general form of operation is not itself an operation or a formal series. It is what *makes possible* the development of formal series. And it is what makes mathematical *constructions* possible. So that in arithmetic we can calculate, and we do not wonder whether the same calculation will always have the same result. We can see that that is how it goes; just as with a periodic decimal, when we see that the remainder is the same as the dividend we can see that it goes on like that.

In the *Tractatus* number is a formal concept or a *form*. We do not learn the meaning of a form as we learn the meaning of a name or a phrase; and I could not explain a form to you as I might explain a general concept. 'Form' and 'construction' go together; and you can understand a construction that is carried out, just as you can understand a sentence, without having anyone tell you what it is. But we could not *define* a propositional form without being circular (the expression for 'the general form of proposition' contains 'elementary proposition'). Neither can we define numbers, in that sense. I say 'in that sense' because Wittgenstein's constructions in 6.02 are definitions in a different sense.

When we are given a formal series we can 'see that it must go on like that'. This is what underlies recursive proofs and definitions. Wittgenstein gives a formal series of definitions by writing the definitions of 1 and 2 and 3 and then writing '(and so on)'. The series develops by the repetition of '+1'; and in this way it shows not only that every number after 1 includes the number which precedes it, but also that the rules for addition—the associative and the commutative laws, for instance—hold for all natural numbers. This means that Wittgenstein is *assuming* arithmetic in order to define number; but this need not be an objection.

He recognized later that he needed brackets if the succession of +1's was to be a formal series. Suppose /, //, ///, ////, /////, with nothing in the signs suggesting the operation by which we get from one of them to another. These signs would not be terms in a formal series. There would be no general term or rule of the series determining the development of it. 'And so on' would mean nothing. But if we write $1+1+1+1+1$ this is just as formless. Unless we have the brackets $((((1)+1)+1)+1)$ how shall we know to what we are adding the next 1?

If Wittgenstein had used brackets in 6.02 the connexion with the repetition of an operation might have seemed less direct. He may also have thought that the 1's should be written without differences in order to show that the brackets are *justified*—to show how repetition of an operation provides for the use of brackets. In 6.231 he says 'It is a property of "$1+1+1+1$" that it can be construed as "$(1+1)+(1+1)$".' It is as though the grammar of '+1' were fundamental for all numerals of the natural numbers. And sometimes when we want to show that it is the same number on each side of the equation, we may feel that to make the demonstration complete we should resolve each numeral into a sum of 1's. This is all right for small numbers. If we write $(1+1)+(1+1+1) = (1+1+1)+(1+1)$ and then drop the brackets we can see that it is the same sign on each side. But if we did this for $18+17 = 17+18$ the substitution of '$1+1+1 \ldots$' would clarify nothing. We should have to count the 1's after the brackets were removed and rely on our original equation. This equation $(18+17 = 17+18)$ is obvious anyway. So why were we inclined to substitute the +1's? Is it a way of showing the general form of addition? of showing *why* the rules of addition hold for all natural numbers? As though that way of writing numerals would show how arithmetic springs from the general form of operation.

In 1923 Skolem spoke of recursive proof of the associative law for addition, for instance. Is Wittgenstein assuming something of the sort when he writes 'and so on' in his definitions with $+1$? Is he assuming that the general form of operation provides it? A little later he would say he was not. But perhaps when he wrote the *Tractatus* he was not clear about it. I suppose the general form of operation (if we want to speak of it) would come in when we have *given* the recursive proof for $a+(b+2)$, $a+(b+3)$, ... and we see that this is a series of proofs having a particular form—a form which holds for all natural numbers. This is not the form of the *recursive* proof; it is what is *shown* in the recursive proof.—If we speak here of drawing a conclusion, then we draw the conclusion from the particular model: the paradigm transition from $a+(b+1) = (a+b)+1$ to the corresponding rule for $a+(b+2)$, say. We do not base anything on the form of calculation in general. And when I said just now that the general form of operation 'would come in when ...', this was not correct; it does not come in at all.

Wittgenstein wanted to show a connexion between arithmetic and the possibility of symbolism. What makes it possible for a symbolism to have sense.

He wanted to forestall the idea that an operation might yield a rigamarole of meaningless signs. Later he wrote of *pseudo-operations*—what look like mathematical operations but are not. It is a pseudo-operation if we cannot see in the signs written down the law or the rule of development which determines them; if the development of a decimal, for instance, is not completely determined by a rule of operation which we know at the start. (In what sense would this be a 'development'?) If it were generally like this—if there were no difference between operation and pseudo-operation—we could not understand any operation. We should not understand the instruction: 'work out the calculation'. The 'so' in 'and so on' would have no meaning.—If this is what 'There is a general form of operation' means, it does not follow that we can ask to have the general form of operation written down. Wittgenstein dropped the whole way of speaking when (in 1929) he gave up speaking of the general form of proposition. But the distinction of operations and truth functions was important in discussing Russell's logical notation for arithmetic. It was perhaps one step towards recognizing that mathematical and logical operations cannot be run together.

4

'The Philosophy of Wittgenstein'

Philosophie versteht niemand: Entweder er versteht nicht, was geschrieben ist; oder er versteht es, aber nicht, daß es Philosophie ist.' *L. Wittgenstein.*

Professor Pitcher* has tried to discuss parts of the *Tractatus* and the *Investigations* sympathetically, and he explains some things that are often misunderstood. But he makes surprising blunders and he is often misleading. He hardly tries to see how the two books are related (perhaps this goes with the distinction he accepts between 'the early Wittgenstein' and 'the later Wittgenstein'). And I think he has missed the *philosophy* of Wittgenstein.

Wittgenstein wanted the two books read together. But this has not helped people to see that the *Investigations* is a book on the philosophy of logic; it has led many, like Pitcher, to read the *Tractatus* as a theory of knowledge. (The Latin title is generally truncated, and no one remembers what Wittgenstein called it.)

When Pitcher is beginning a short note (pp. 63–5) on the role of the Sheffer stroke in the *Tractatus* view of general propositions, he says: 'This note can be omitted by those readers with no elementary knowledge of logic.' But how can such readers understand the *Tractatus* at all? What understanding will Pitcher's book give them? He does not show the importance of logical form and of symbolism. He concentrates on 'the picture theory', but because he neglects logical form he misses the sense of it. He shows no sense of the difficulties involved in any attempt to give an account of logic—although these are the theme of the *Investigations* too. He does not try to compare the different ideas of analysis in the earlier book and the later one.

* *The Philosophy of Wittgenstein.* By George Pitcher. (Englewood Cliffs, N.J.: Prentice-Hall Inc., 1964.)

Maybe too much has been written on the *Tractatus*: when it becomes a subject for commentaries, Wittgenstein's own expressions of his thoughts are muffled, and students will hardly sense what he is doing. If you do not see how style or force of expression are important you cannot see how Wittgenstein thought of philosophical difficulties and of philosophical method.

Wittgenstein says in the *Tractatus* that propositions are truth functions of elementary propositions, and Pitcher finds this 'an extraordinary, one almost wants to say, an incredible thesis' (p. 67). To explain his holding it he suggests that 'Wittgenstein first arrived at a theory—call it X—which he thought was necessarily true. Theory X entailed the view that propositions are *truth functions* of elementary propositions; it demanded that this theory of truth functions be true. Then finally Wittgenstein considered all the types of propositions that he could think of, and tried to account for them all, in one way or another, on his theory of truth functions. ... Theory X ... is Wittgenstein's famous picture theory of propositions.'

The 'thesis' was pretty well developed in the 1913 *Notes on Logic*, and in the 1914 *Notes Dictated to Moore*, before Wittgenstein had started to speak of propositions as 'picturing'. But in any case, when Pitcher refers to 'all the types of propositions that he could think of' he misses the sense of 'all' that is relevant to the discussion of 'the general form of proposition'. He misses the distinction between what is called in 6.031 'die *zufällige* Allgemeinheit' and the generality proper to logic and mathematics, i.e., the generality of a variable. 4.53 reads: 'The general propositional form is a variable', and 'A proposition is a truth-function of elementary propositions' follows immediately on this.

The general form of logical operation is the general rule for the construction of *all* propositions since 'we cannot think illogically'. Pitcher leaves the notion of 'thinking' or 'act of thinking' vague in a way the *Tractatus* would not have allowed. For the general form of logical operation is the general form of thinking: and thinking is calculating.

When we read the *Tractatus* it seems as though the structure of a *Sachverhalt* must yield the symbolic representation of it by a logical rule or 'translation'. Wittgenstein sometimes spoke of a formal operation (in a calculus) as a 'translation' of one formula into another. He also said that you might produce a painting from the description of a scene, so that the painting was a translation of the description. This is part of what he meant by the *Bildhaftigkeit der Sprache*. Here we could substitute a copy of the painting and it would do as well. Similarly, if you 'describe' a proposition you are repeating it; to 'describe' a calculation would be to repeat the calculation, and so on. (Whereas in describing an experiment you are not repeating the experiment.)

This possibility of 'translation' is a logical or internal relation. And it is misleading to say, as Pitcher does (p. 88 and elsewhere), that for Wittgenstein 'correlating elements of a picture (or proposition) with elements of reality is a mental act—the mental act namely of meaning or intending the former to stand for the latter'. No doubt the names we use are conventional; but this is one of the reasons for speaking of 'das *eigentliche* Zeichen'—and without this notion there would be nothing for the mental act to intend.

See the words in their possible uses (in their *sinnvollen Gebrauch*), and you see in them the form of logical operation. 5.47 says that 'in fact elementary propositions themselves contain all logical operations'. And 5.4733, in almost the same sense: 'When [the word 'identical'] appears as a sign of equality, it symbolizes in a different way—the signifying relation is a different one. . . .' The relation of a sign to what it signifies is the same as the relation of signs to one another in a particular calculus.

Wittgenstein expresses this clearly in 3.11: 'We treat the perceptible sign of a proposition (what is spoken or written, etc.) as a projection of a possible situation.' And the same passage continues: 'Die Projektionsmethode ist das Denken des Satz-Sinnes.' In other words, the method of projection is what we *mean* by 'thinking' or 'understanding' the sense of the proposition. (Messrs Pears and McGuiness read it differently, as though the remark were to explain the expression 'method of projection' here. I do not think this fits with what follows. And I think 'projection', which is a logical operation, is written to explain 'das Denken des Satz-Sinnes'. The 'ist' after 'Projektions-methode' might have been italicized.)

'Propositions are pictures' is itself *ein Bild* in the sense of Maxwell's models. To see how it was meant we have to look at the rest of the *Tractatus*. 2.1 says 'Wir machen uns Bilder der

Tatsachen' (perhaps: 'We construct pictures of facts'), and the next sentence is: 'The construction represents a situation in logical space, the existence and non-existence of states of affairs.' This shows what is *meant* by picturing facts to ourselves: constructing a situation in logical space; or we might say, seeing it in a system. There is no *other* way of picturing a fact.

Since Pitcher hardly considers internal relations he does not ask what they are contrasted with. He says (p. 73) that for Wittgenstein states of affairs are 'entirely independent of one another'. Of course they are *logically* independent; but this does not mean they are unrelated. 5.42 says that Russell's symbols for logical constants are not relations in the sense in which 'right' and 'left' are; they do not *signify* relations. But it is clear all through the *Tractatus* that states of affairs do stand in spatial relations to one another, and that states of affairs arise after others and before the states of affairs that succeed them. Assigning causes to events belongs to a definite description of them (6.3611, 6.362 and elsewhere). Nothing Wittgenstein says would imply that experiments do not teach us anything or that experimental physicists are being superstitious. The superstition would lie in imagining a hidden connexion behind what we observe, or in thinking that what happens is a consequence of natural laws.

If Wittgenstein had spoken as Pitcher supposes, he would have been saying we cannot describe what there is and what happens. But then there would be no logic.

The question '*How* is the picture connected with the fact it pictures?' can only mean: 'How does it have the role of a picture at all?' If 'I' were to perform the mental act or intention of correlating the marks or sounds with elements of a fact, this would not make the complex a picture. I cannot 'correlate' unless I am working *with* a picture. And then the 'correlating' means simply that the syntax of the picture shows the possible structure of a fact. The relations of logical syntax are internal relations, and they make it possible to introduce conventional signs. ('Only in the connexion of a proposition does a name have meaning.')

Pitcher's neglect of formal series and of the general form of logical operation makes it hard for him to understand what is meant by 'the limits of language' or 'the limits of the world'.

'Solipsism' illustrates a tendency or an attempt to say what

can mean nothing at all. If Wittgenstein had meant that 'solipsism is trying to say something true' (Pitcher, p. 144), the discussion he gives would be pointless. What solipsism brings out is
that there *are* limits to language. And this is like 'saying' that we
cannot think illogically.

Suppose that in trying to express solipsism he speaks of 'the
only language I understand'. Obviously he is not confessing his
limited command of languages; he is not speaking of what *he*
can understand. If he speaks of what is possible and what is
impossible in language, the word 'I' will not come in. Nor is he
voicing a relativism which says, 'of course in another language
it might be different'. 'Another language' would be an illogical
language—which means nothing.

If solipsism 'wants to say' that I cannot contrast the intelligibility I know with the intelligibility of a higher language—all right, except that this is empty. 'Intelligible only in a
higher language' means nothing. (This is how the distinction
of what can be said and what can be shown dismisses the theory
of types. Cf. D. S. Shwayder, *Inquiry*, Volume 7, 1964.)

Neither here nor elsewhere, apparently, does Pitcher see that
Wittgenstein is speaking of constant *tendencies* in our language.
He thinks that at the end of the book, in 6.54, Wittgenstein is
saying of his propositions what he has said about solipsism.
Whereas the tendency to solipsism is an example of what *calls*
for the remarks of the *Tractatus*. Certainly solipsism is not an
elucidation in the way Wittgenstein's propositions are.

When Wittgenstein said 'Meine Sätze erläutern dadurch, daß
sie der, welcher mich versteht, am Ende als unsinnig erkennt,
wenn er durch sie—auf ihnen—über sie hinausgestiegen ist'—
he was not saying they were metaphysical. Otherwise they would
not 'erläutern', nor could anyone understand them—as he must,
before he can see them (in the special sense suggested) as nonsensical. Later Wittgenstein did recognize that important
features of the *Tractatus* are metaphysical. But this is not his
point in 6.54.

Pitcher shows less understanding still when he tries to speak
of 'what is mystical'. (Not a translation of 'das Mystische', but
there is none.) I doubt if there has been an intelligent discussion
of this. But no one who understood the rest of the *Tractatus*
would join the comments of what Pitcher calls 'the tough-
minded men of the Vienna Circle'. As though Wittgenstein had

kept to rigorous thinking less than Neurath did. Or Ayer. Du lieber Gott.

Pitcher thinks that 'what is mystical' for Wittgenstein was something lying *beyond* what can be expressed. There is not only the world we can describe; there is also 'the jungle' (p. 161), 'and one has the feeling that Wittgenstein longs to escape into parts of it from the city in which he has imprisoned us all'. 'The jungle cannot actually be seen ... the darkness of something unthinkable.' (Imagine what Wittgenstein would have said to *that* utterance.)

Yet Pitcher never mentions the two most important propositions which have to do with 'what is mystical'. I mean 6.44 and 6.522:

6.44: 'What is mystical is not the *character* of the world, but *that* there is a world'—i.e., that there is anything at all. This should be taken with 5.552: 'The "experience" that we need in order to understand logic is not that something is in such and such a state, but that something *is*: and this is *not* an experience.' Try translating this into 'the darkness of something unthinkable'.

6.522: 'No doubt there is what cannot be expressed. This *shows* itself, it is what is mystical.' This is not something which 'cannot actually be seen'. It is closely related with the remark about the logical properties of language, which Pitcher had quoted some pages earlier from the *Notes Dictated to Moore*. And it *shows* itself precisely *in* the rigorous use of language, in saying what can be expressed. The distinction of what can and what cannot be expressed has no analogy with the difference between light and darkness.

I do not think Pitcher ever saw what kind of questioning led Wittgenstein to write the *Tractatus*; nor what it was Wittgenstein hoped others might learn from it. So the closing remarks mean little to him. What sort of solution do they suggest? What deep-going difficulties could be met in this way?

The *Investigations* might have helped him. But he sees Wittgenstein here demolishing his earlier system and erecting a new one (p. 187). Whereas Wittgenstein would have demolished, if he could, the idea of philosophical discussion as a contest to settle who's right and who's wrong.

Long before the *Investigations* he was telling his students: 'What I should like to get at is for you not to agree with me in particular opinions but to investigate the matter in the right way. To notice the interesting kind of thing (that is, the things which will serve as keys if you use them properly). . . . I don't want to give you a definition of philosophy, but I should like you to have a very lively idea as to the characters of philosophical problems. If you had, by the way, I could stop lecturing at once. . . . What I want to teach you isn't opinions but a method. In fact the method to treat as irrelevant every question of opinions. . . . If I'm wrong then you are right, which is just as good. As long as you look for the same thing. . . . I don't try to make you *believe* something you *don't* believe, but to make you *do* something you won't do.' And a few years later: 'What we are trying to learn is a way of investigating certain problems. A way of investigating which goes very much *against the grain* of some people.' He emphasized again and again that it is hard to understand a philosophical problem in its depth: to keep from short-circuiting, from superficial solutions.

In *Investigations* §81 he says he must discuss the concepts of understanding, meaning and thinking, if he is to show how language may delude one into thinking that 'if anyone utters a sentence and *means* it, or *understands* it, he is working with a calculus according to strict rules'. What he says of 'private experience' or 'private language' is part of this, and belongs to the discussion of 'following a rule'.

He had begun the passage (§81) with a remark of Ramsey's, and it was often with Ramsey in mind that he wrote of grammatical rules and empirical propositions. Ramsey had criticized Wittgenstein for 'treating what is vague as if it were precise and trying to fit it into an exact logical category' ('Last Papers' in *The Foundations of Mathematics*, p. 269). Wittgenstein came to see the mistake of treating the concepts of 'proposition' and of 'understanding' as though they were not vague. But Ramsey, he thought, had never recognized the problem—had not seen what the issues were—in showing the relation of this vagueness to logical exactitude. Ramsey was inclined to make logic an empirical science (cf. op. cit., pp. 267, 268): 'It seems to me that in the process of our thought . . . we are forced to look not only at the object which we are talking about, but at our own mental states. . . . [A solution in philosophy] will have something of the nature of a hypothesis, for we shall accept it not as the consequence of direct argument but as the only one we can think of which satisfied our several requirements. . . . We are in the ordinary position of scientists having to be content with piece-meal improvements. . . .' As though he were bringing together the exactitude of logic and the exactitude—or *accuracy*—of science. This mistakes philosophical discussion. For what we need in philosophy is *conceptual* analysis of 'mental states' (not our *own* mental states)—not a hypothesis based on *observation* of them. This is a grammatical investigation; an investigation of the ways we use these concepts, of the language games into which they come. 'We are not analysing a phenomenon (thinking, for instance) but a concept (say the concept of thinking), i.e. the use of a word' (§382). And (discussing the notion of 'imagining that someone is in pain', §392): ' "When I imagine he's in pain, what goes on in me is really just. . . ." And then someone says: "I believe I can imagine it even *without* thinking that . . .". ("I believe I can think without speaking.") This leads nowhere. It fluctuates between a scientific analysis and a grammatical one.' Unless we keep them apart—unless we see how they differ—we shall not see what logic is.

After his discussions with Ramsey—it was after Ramsey's death I think—he dropped the idea that logic must have the 'perfect' exactitude of an ideal. Its real exactitude does not lie that way, any more than in scientific accuracy. 'Get back to rough ground'—look to actual examples and learn from them. The examples describe what happens; instead of justifying or explaining it. You describe my *means* of examples. Not as if you were describing a particular happening (as you might describe a battle); you are describing a *practice*. The examples themselves tell of happenings there and then, but we speak of these places and times 'as we speak of the pieces of chess when we are listing the rules of the game, not when we are describing their physical properties' (§108).

Can one describe a rule? How would this differ from the empirical proposition that people follow a rule in this and this way?

In philosophy we do not try to explain something unfamiliar and yet the trouble does come from the subject matter. Grammatical rules and propositions are immensely important in all that we say: 'there would be no language at all without them'. But when we realize this it is easy to move to a wrong idea of the logic of language—we misunderstand the sense of the remark

that without propositions and rules it would not be *language*—
and we feel the propositions have some remarkable properties
or powers (§93).

Show how rules of grammar are rules of the lives in which
there is language; and show at the same time that rules have
not the role of empirical statements. This is not asking us to
show that they are *really* rules—that we are justified in following
them. (Like establishing the certainty of mathematics.) We are
not asking *why* our language has this grammar. 'Keep from
asking "why", and simply *describe*'—remembering that this is
not a description of anyone's mental experiences.

And yet in this sort of description we have to ask, apparently,
'What is *mathematical* in this expression?' or 'What shows that
this is the statement of a rule?' Which seems half-way to asking
'What does it have to be if it is to be a rule of grammar?'—
showing that we have left the rough ground.

(Wie weit kann man die Funktion der Regel beschrei-
ben? Wer noch keine beherrscht, den kann ich nur abrich-
ten. Aber wie kann ich mir selbst das Wesen der Regel
erklären?

Das Schwere ist hier nicht bis auf den Grund zu graben,
sondern den Grund, der vor uns liegt, als Grund erkennen.

Denn der Grund spiegelt mir immer wieder eine größere
Tiefe vor, und wenn wir diese zu erreichen suchen, finden
wir uns immer wieder auf dem alten Niveau.

Unsere Krankheit ist die, erklären zu wollen.)

Wittgenstein speaks of 'temptations' we feel in reflecting on
language, and especially on logic. (Perhaps we keep wondering
whether the grammar and the concepts we use allow us to
grasp things as they really are, for instance.) But he is not
saying something about human nature, or the special weak-
nesses of those who do philosophy. He sometimes spoke of
analogies between philosophy and psychoanalysis, but these are
analogies in *method*. The functional disorders which philosophy
treats appear as delusions and dreams of our language (§358).
And what he says about 'tackling' philosophical difficulties
might suggest, again and again, some analogy with treatment.
To root out the difficulty we have to start thinking about these
things in a new way; you have to call to mind something you

have been doing all along—something which (for special reasons) it is *hard* to call to mind; you have to bring together practices you know and take for granted, so that each of them appears in a different light; and this cannot be done all at once: we are concerned with problems whose answer you cannot reach just by thinking, but through practice; 'I am not trying to make you believe something you don't believe, but to get you to do something you won't do.' When Wittgenstein spoke of Hilbert's remark that 'no one shall drive us from the Heaven which Cantor has created for us', he said 'I would never dream of trying to drive anyone from any Heaven. I would try to do something quite different: to show that it isn't Heaven. And then you'll leave of your own accord.'

But in other ways his methods were not at all like pyscho-analysis. If it is hard to recall certain features of the language I constantly use, then obviously this is not because of incidents in my personal history. No more than I'd have 'got rid of' a philosophical difficulty if I happened to lose interest and stopped bothering about it. In many ways Wittgenstein's methods are more like certain general methods of mathematicians. The main point is that the discussions in the *Investigations* are meant to illuminate—throw a different light on—certain expressions which we use. The character of these discussions—the order and relevance of the remarks—depends on this. By following them we may come to see what logic is—what 'internal relations' are, for instance. Neither Ramsey's empirical methods nor methods of formal proof could help us here. (I do not mean that the *Investigations* is trying to demonstrate that 'this is the only method'. The discussions are illustrations of it—are exercises in conceptual analysis.)

I have said '*certain* expressions', and I mean for instance: 'language', 'proposition', 'sense (and nonsense)', 'rule', 'reason', 'understanding', 'thinking', 'reality', 'must', 'can'. . . . There are special sorts of trouble which I meet when I try to think out or explain the meaning of any of these. For example, the fact that I have to use the expression itself in explaining it. Wittgenstein uses the notion of 'family likeness' among various 'language games' both to bring out these difficulties and to dispel them. Pitcher remarks (at considerable length) that there are many other expressions, such as 'lemon' and 'sitting down', which could be said to apply to 'a family of cases' and which are

not precisely defined; as though this were the same point. No
doubt there are analogies; no doubt you could talk about family
likenesses in still other connexions. But Pitcher has not understood the special use which Wittgenstein makes of the notion
here.

Wittgenstein remarked once that we might say we have a
strictly defined concept of multiplication in cardinal arithmetic—that this covers a strictly limited set of operations, even
though there is no finite number of multiplications in this
arithmetic. And he said that we have *no* such concept of
'mathematics' or of 'language'. Yet in the *Tractatus* he had
thought we did: 'proposition' and 'language' were strictly
limited in much the same way as 'multiplication' is. The limit
is given in the general form of operation. And in this sense he
could speak of the limits of language, and of the meaningless-
ness which comes from trying to overstep them.

Even ten years after the *Tractatus* was published he would say
that the grammar of 'language' 'muß im vornhinein bestimmt
sein und hängt nicht von irgendeinem künftigen Ereignis ab',
although it was not determined by the general form of truth
functions. We could say that someone knows the grammar of
'language', or knows what language is, if he has learned to
speak. He has an idea of what it makes sense to ask, or what it
makes sense to say. (It would mean nothing to speak of his
'trying to understand' any and every jumble of sounds or
marks.) If we can speak, we can tell the difference between
sense and nonsense—we can understand the question *whether*
this or that makes sense—and it would mean nothing to say
that future experiments may show that our ideas of sense and
nonsense are all wrong. The experiments could not show us
anything (i.e., they would not be experiments) unless we could
describe them and understand the reports of them. (New developments in mathematics might make new experiments possible, but not the other way about.)

But this still seems like saying that knowing the grammar of
'language' or knowing the grammar of 'proposition' is—in
some way—the same as knowing the grammars of this, that and
the other proposition. And Wittgenstein asked 'Wie verhält sich
die Grammatik des Wortes "Satz" zur Grammatik der Sätze?'

The trouble lies, apparently, in speaking of '*die* Grammatik
des Wortes "Satz" '; and analogously for 'language'. But when

we say this we are recognizing new problems. 'There are various grammars' may look like 'There are different varieties of lemons' or (though this is different) 'There are various forms of calculation in arithmetic.' Yet neither of these comes near to what Wittgenstein was saying when (in reference to 'What is language?') he spoke of various language games. For it is not just that one system may have a different grammar from another—as chess has different rules from draughts. We feel like saying that 'grammar' *means* something different in one game ('system of communication') and in another; that the sense of 'rule' is different in this connexion and in that—not 'the rules are different'.

Yet we use the same word; and this, the word—like the word 'Satz'—is what we want to understand. To say it covers a family of cases does not mean just that if you thought of the grammar (or the rules) of sea-side banter you would not ask the kind of questions you might in speaking of the rules of legal evidence. These words—'proposition' (or 'sentence' or 're-mark'), 'grammar', 'rule', 'proof' and so on—have their meanings in particular surroundings or environments. You say you are listening to a remark, or looking at the sentence that has been written here. But if you heard this (what you are listening to) in circumstances in which it could have no connexion, even through history, with the lives of people who speak with one another, you would not call it a remark. In a calculation we pass from certain symbolic expressions to others, and there are regularities in the ways in which we do this: we say we are guided by what the constituent signs allow. In the established practice or technique of mathematics we call this calculation. Otherwise— if there were no mathematics, or if you had no idea that there was—I could not say I had illustrated 'calculation' for you. You would not grasp what I meant by 'regularities' when I tried to point them out to you. I cannot begin explaining with: 'Look, *this* is a calculation', even if I know you will pay close attention.

Wittgenstein illustrates this with the word 'reading'; which we might contrast with words like 'staring' or 'jumping' (or 'sitting down'). We cannot say the man is reading except in connexion with certain ways of living: where people inscribe monuments, post public proclamations, keep records, write reports, write letters, etc., etc. And there need be nothing like this with 'staring' or 'jumping'. If I tell you the snake is staring at something, you will know what I mean, but not if I tell you the snake is reading.

We could not teach someone what 'reading' means by pointing to examples, as we might in explaining 'jumping' or 'sitting down' or 'lemon'. And you cannot learn to read—as you might learn to somersault—by imitating what someone else is doing. (A child may teach itself to read—but not that way.) This has led to the idea that 'reading', 'understanding', 'meaning', 'thinking', 'wishing', 'deciding' . . . are all of them learned indirectly, since we cannot point to what is really meant.

And it is true that we cannot point to what is really meant. But not because it is hidden from us. It is hard to give an account of 'reading', for instance, because its *meaning* lies in the language game in which we use it. As one cannot say this about 'sitting down'. All the puzzling words we study here are words having to do with the grammar of 'language'.

If someone hears the word 'spectroscope' for the first time and asks me what it means—I might be able to tell him something about it. But if a man heard the word 'reading' for the first time—someone from a land where there was no reading—and asked me 'What is reading?' . . . Or suppose you wanted to convey to a wolf-boy that you were speaking to him.

'What is speaking?' is very like 'What is time?' And if, when someone asks, you cannot answer, it is the varied family of games which are the use of the word—'time' no less than 'speaking'—which gives trouble. (People find 'time' baffling for different reasons and in different connexions. I am not trying to say: 'What makes "time" baffling is . . .') We cannot enumerate and say '*these* are all the language games which belong to the grammar of "time" '. It may never have struck me before that some form of language—say geometry—does or could belong to the 'meaning' of 'time'. (Which helps to show the sense of 'Don't look for the meaning, look at the use.') This is not like the uncertainty of borderline or doubtful cases—'Would you still call that a dwelling house?', 'Would you still call that a fruit?' —where the answer may be: 'As you like.'

Suppose that in the language of some society there is a word or a way of speaking which corresponds to a part of what we might call using the concept of time; but that there was nothing corresponding to what *we* might call 'all the rest that comes into the meaning of "time" '. It would be a mistake if we said that their language was *incomplete* since there are so many properties of time of which it can give no account. If I had asked you to give an account of our use of 'time' and you mentioned only those ways of speaking which have counterparts in that other language your account would be incomplete. But it may help us to understand 'language' and to understand 'time' if we recognize that there might be a language *without* many of the techniques and applications which have grown into our time grammar (cf. *Investigations* §497).

This 'anthropological' view (anthropologische Betrachtungs-weise) is an important feature of the method of discussion or analysis in the *Investigations*. I do not think we can understand the use of the notion of 'family likenesses among language games' if we neglect it. (Naturally, the phrase 'anthropologische Betrachtungsweise' has itself been misunderstood; perhaps because philosophers pay little attention to *Investigations* II, xii—p. 230.) Wittgenstein remarked once (during the latter years of his work on the *Investigations*): 'Der Vorteil der Betrachtung der Sprachspiele ist eben, daß sie uns *stufenweise* erblicken läßt, was wir sonst nur in einem *einzigen*—verworrenen Knäuel sehen.' But this kind of analysis through language games is meant for those expressions which seem in a special way grammatical—'rule', 'proposition', 'understanding' . . .—or which seem to be aspects of what we mean by 'language'. The confusion we meet when we try to explain them is a confusion *within* what we mean by them, a confusion regarding certain forms of language or of understanding. This is what makes the description of a language game—perhaps contrasting it with others which we have invented just for the sake of the contrast—so helpful.

(We should not have to describe a whole language game, or a series of language games, in order to bring out the variations in what we mean by 'lemon'.)

We are no longer comparing different ways of saying the same thing (as in the *Tractatus*). We are comparing different ways of speaking or carrying on discourse with one another, and in this sense different languages. And the point is not to see what is common to them all; very often it is just the opposite: to see that there need be nothing common to them all. Which is harder than you think.

It means, for example, that there might be two languages which were not translatable into one another. Not because there was no key, but because any 'key' by which you thought you had rendered their speech in our language would have changed their form of communication (Form der menschlichen Verständigung) into something it was not.

What bothers then is the question of what makes it a *language*. If we cannot even grasp what distinguishing sense and nonsense would be in their case—docs this mean that *our* distinction is just arbitrary or relative? Wittgenstein remarks (§520): '... "Also hängt es ganz von unserer Grammatik ab, was (logisch) möglich genannt wird, und was nicht,—nämlich eben was sie zuläßt?"—Aber das ist doch willkürlich!—Ist es willkürlich? —Nicht mit jeder Satzartigen Bildung wissen wir etwas anzufangen, nicht jede Technik hat eine Verwendung in userm Leben, und wenn wir in der Philosophie versucht sind, etwas ganz Unnützes unter die Satze zu zählen, so geschieht es oft, weil wir uns seine Anwendung nicht genügend überlegt haben.' And in a context analogous to this in the *Remarks on the Foundations of Mathematics*, page 180: 'Mathematik ist also eine Familie; aber das sagt nicht, daß es uns also gleich sein wird, was alles in sie aufgenommen wird.' We may feel that this still leaves it relative. If the question whether this is an intelligible expression—and especially, the question whether this is logically possible—depends on whether it 'has an application in our life', this seems to take all the force out of logic, and out of language. But here the trouble is partly that we have not understood (or have not kept in mind) the sense of '*application* in our life' of which Wittgenstein is speaking; and partly from confusions about the 'generality' (as opposed to 'relativity') of logic, or of language.

In *The Blue Book* (pp. 18, 19) Wittgenstein spoke of a special form of the craving for generality as 'the real source of metaphysics'. He added: 'Instead of "craving for generality" I could also have said "the contemptuous attitude towards the particular case ...". The contempt for what seems the less general case in logic springs from the idea that it is incomplete. It is in fact confusing to talk of cardinal arithmetic as something special as opposed to something more general. Cardinal arithmetic bears no marks of incompleteness. ....' Pitcher prefers, he says (p. 198 and ff.), to talk of 'craving for unity'—as though this were just a happier wording of the same idea. But a craving for unity is not at all the same as a craving for *completeness*. Wittgenstein is speaking of *logical* completeness; the completeness of a logical system—where it *can* also be spoken of as generality. A craving for some guarantee that the different parts of mathematics are not just arbitrary techniques; a craving for some guarantee that the methods we have formulated will not be upset by the appearance of some case for which they have not provided. The generality of the *foundations*. This is a form of what the *Investigations* calls 'eine Tendenz, die Logik unserer Sprache zu sublimieren' (§38).

Is a system of calculations arbitrary as long as you could imagine other systems or other forms of calculation not derivable from these axioms? 'Arbitrary' is taken to imply that it would not really have the force of a calculation. But what could '*really* have the force' mean here? If it *has* the force of a calculation in the use that is made of it, what *else* could it have? (This is the sense of 'Verwendung in unserm Leben'.) Wittgenstein's investigation is meant to bring out what we do mean by the force of a calculation, or by mathematical necessity; to consider, for example, under what circumstances we ever do use these expressions, and what we are trying to do, what the point is, when we do: to make clear their Sprachlogik—or to make clear the 'civil status' ('die bürgerliche Stellung') of mathematical necessity. Cf. §125.

If we said that our language, or any language that people speak, is 'arbitrary'—are we considering the possibility that it may not really be a language after all? although people do speak it, understand one another, etc.? When we say 'There must be some form of intelligibility which is not accidental, which does not vary with the lives and customs of peoples', we are trying to come out of some unclarity about the intelligibility with which *we* have to do in the language we speak. And it is pretty obvious that:

(a) we have no idea what relation such a form of intelligibility (or logical structure) might have to our language. To say 'its being a language *depends* on that' is empty—ein Scheingesims;

(b) if we discovered, or if it were proved, that there *is* no such form of intelligibility, this would make no difference whatever to the way we distinguish between sense and nonsense, the ways in which we try to determine what is meant, our criteria for saying that he has mistaken the meaning, etc., etc. (Any more than discovering contradictions in the foundations of mathematics would make any difference to the way we do cardinal arithmetic.)

It is the same if we say that the measure of what can be understood is in 'the language of our thoughts'—that everything is built on this. It seems natural at first to say that I can put words together in a meaningless combination, but that I cannot put ideas together to form a meaningless idea. (*Investigations* §512) 'Ideas have their own grammar, not one that is learned', etc. What we say or write means something sometimes; and sometimes only seems to. Without the language of ideas *this* distinction—between a genuine remark and what only seems like one—were empty, and there would be no language.

But this view crumbles if you study it. The two remarks Wittgenstein makes in §512 are enough. There is no reason to say that I could not have a nonsensical or impossible idea. Anyway, no such language of ideas comes into the methods by which we decide whether what has been said here is nonsense or not. It cannot help to show, for instance, whether the question 'Are there 777 in the development of π?' has sense. (§§516, 517.)

Pitcher speaks of some of this in his chapter on 'Sensations and the Talk of Them'. He speaks of the language game or grammar in which we talk of physical objects, and the different grammar in which we talk of personal experiences. But he is interested in this as a special development in the theory of knowledge. And Wittgenstein's discussion was something different. Of course Wittgenstein dwells on those differences of grammar. But one reason why he turns from so many angles to what we say of sensations and feelings is that these are often run together with a notion of 'private experience' that is confused and is supposed to do for speech and understanding what sensations and feelings could never do. Throughout, he is talking of 'following a rule' and of the tendency to think I must have a *justification* for speaking as I do—as though it meant anything to speak of what justifies me in calling this postage stamp blue (cf. §§239, 240). (A formal proof in mathematics may justify me in taking the result as a rule—i.e., as a proposition in mathematics. And there may be a formal check or test of the proof. Here Wittgenstein would ask 'When—under what circumstances

—do you *call* this a test?'—imagining somewhat different circumstances in which you would no longer call it that. Within our mathematics this *is* a test—that is all.) Questions concerning the 'interpretation' of symbolic expressions are connected with this: with the question whether we are justified in following the rule in this way. The last two paragraphs of *Investigations* Part I (§§692, 693) give what has been the theme from §81 onwards.

Pitcher hardly mentions Part II. If he had studied II, xii— the most important short statement for an understanding of the book—he might have seen how far it is from anything J. L. Austin was doing.

5

Can there be a Private Language?*

The problem about private languages is the problem of how words mean. This is much the same as the question of what a rule of language is.

When we talk about something, our language does not point to it, nor mirror it. Pointing or mirroring could refer to things only within a convention, anyway: only when there is a way in which pointing is understood and a way in which mirroring is understood. I point for the sake of someone who understands it. Apart from that it were an idle ceremony; as idle as making sounds in front of things.

Our words refer to things by the way they enter in discourse; by their connexions with what people are saying and doing, for instance, and by the way they affect what is said and done. What we say makes a difference. What expressions we use makes a difference. And the notion of a rule goes with that. If it made no difference what sound you made or when, you could not be understood and you would have said nothing. If you have said something, your utterance will be taken in one way and not in another. In many cases you will have committed yourself to saying other things, to answering in certain ways if you are asked, or to doing certain things. That belongs to the regular use of your words, and that is why it would not have been just the same if you had used others instead. That is also why it is possible to learn the language.

When we speak of 'use' we may think of general practice and we may think of rules. Sometimes these can be left together, but sometimes there are differences we ought to notice. When I learn the use of an expression, or learn what it means—that is

* From a symposium with A. J. Ayer, 1954.

how other people speak. Yet I do not say I have learned what other people do; I have learned what it means. I may learn what it means *by* observing what other people do, and of course if I know what it means I know that others who speak the language will use it in that way. But I have not learned what generally happens. I have learned a rule.

That is in some ways like learning the rules of a game, although in some ways it is very different. It is different from learning the rules of a calculus, too. In fact in some ways it is misleading to talk of rules at all here. But it does make some things clearer—that it is possible to use an expression wrongly, for instance.

A rule is something that is *kept*. That is why we can know what we are talking about. When you have learned how the expression is used, then you can not merely behave as other people do, you can also *say* something. That is not a matter of behaving in a particular way. 'This is red' does not mean 'Everyone calls this red'. If that were all there were to it nothing would mean anything.

And yet, that there should be rules at all does depend on what people do, and on an agreement in what they do. If you teach someone the meaning of a colour word by showing him samples of the colour, then he will probably understand; and if he understands he will go on to use the word in new situations just as you would. If he remembered your instruction all right but differed wildly from you in what he called 'the same as' the samples you had shown him, and if this went on no matter how often you repeated your explanation, then he could never learn what that colour word means. And this holds generally, not just with colours. It is a point to which Wittgenstein is referring in *Investigations* §242. Of course that situation practically never arises. And if it were at all general we could not speak.

I am not saying, 'People see that their reactions tally, and this makes communication possible.' That would assume considerable understanding and language already. The agreement of which I am speaking is something without which it would not be possible for people to 'see' that their reactions tallied or that anything else tallied. We see that we understand one another, without noticing whether our reactions tally or not. *Because* we agree in our reactions, it is possible for me to tell you something, and it is possible for you to teach me something.

56

The consensus of reactions is in this sense prior to language, but the reactions themselves are not languages, nor are they language. Neither does the agreement in reactions come first or anticipate language. It appears as the language does, it is a common way of taking the expressions of the language. They are common reactions within the course of language—not to anything there might have been before language or apart from it.

Because there is this agreement we can understand one another. And since we understand one another we have rules. We might perhaps speak of being 'trusted' to go on in the way that is for us the only natural one. But if you have learned the language you take it for granted. If anyone did not, we could never understand him.

Because there is this agreement it is possible to say something. When I tell you that the patch on the patient's skin is red, I am not saying that it is called red, but that it *is* red. But I could mean nothing definite by that, and you could not understand me, unless people who have learned the words as we have would agree in calling this red. If people could not be brought to use the word in any regular way, if one man who had been taught as we have should go on to give the name to what we should call the complementary colour, if another used it as we do on Monday but in a different way on Tuesday, and if others did not show even these degrees of regularity—then it would not mean anything to say that someone had used the word mistakenly. There would be no distinction between mistakenly and correctly. And there would be no distinction between saying that it is red and saying anything else.

It is not a statement about what I do or about what people generally do. But unless the words had a regular use I should not know it was red, and I should not know what colour it was, because there would be nothing to know. I know what colour it is because I know red when I see it; I know what red is. A bull may charge at a red flag, and rats may be trained to react in one way to red lights and in another way to blue lights, but neither the bull nor the rat knows what red is, and neither knows that this is red. We might put this by saying that neither of them has the concept 'red' and neither of them has the concept 'colour'. No one can get the concept of colour just by looking at colours, or of red just by looking at red things. If I have the concept, I know how the word 'red' is used. There must *be* a use, though;

57

there must be what I have been calling common reactions. The phrase 'the same colour' must mean something and be generally understood, and also 'a different colour'. I must know when it makes sense to talk about different shades of the same colour; and so on. Unless I did know what it makes sense to say, unless I were used to talking about colours and to understanding people when they did, then I should not know what red is and I should not know red when I see it.

Of course the colour red is not the word 'red'. And I suppose if a man cannot see hc will never know what it is. But the colour red is not *this*, either. This is red. But if I say 'This is the *colour* red', that is a definition—I am giving you a definition by showing you a sample. And the point of that depends upon the definition's being taken in a particular way; and also on its connexion with other uses of language. If I had just shown you that sample without saying anything, and without your asking —what would you have learned from this? Not what the colour red is, anyway.

Someone might say, 'I know what *I* mean by "red". It is what I experience when I look at this. Whether I have this experience under the same circumstances as lead you to use the word—that is a further question, which may be important in deciding the description of physical objccts. But I know what colour *I* see in these circumstances.' (It would be hard to keep from asking, 'Well, what colour *do* you see?') I suppose the point would be that I know this independently of having learned the (public) language. If I know what I mean, in this way—if I know what colour *I* am referring to—then apparently I have done something like giving myself a definition. But I must also have confused giving a definition and following a definition. It is this which allows me to evade the difficulty of what I am going to *call* 'following the definition'. Which is a real difficulty: what could it mean to say that I had followed the definition— 'my' definition—incorrectly? But if that has no sense, then what on earth is the point of the definition? And what does the definition *establish*?

Suppose someone asked 'What colour is red?' and thought it was like asking 'What colour is blood?' This, he might think, is something which I can learn only by my own experience, my immediate experience. And although I can tell you what colour blood is, I cannot tell you what colour red is. I can only suggest things that may enable you to find out for yourself. Well, but in this case what is the sense of 'what colour red *is*'? If it is something nobody can say, then nobody can ask it either. Suppose I ask it only of myself—but whatever is it I am asking? Something I should like to know? But if that has no sense, then there is nothing I tell myself either. Perhaps I say 'What a colour!', but that is all.

I cannot learn the colour unless I can see it; but I cannot learn it without language either. I know it because I know the language. And it is similar with sensations. I know a headache when I feel it, and I know I felt giddy yesterday afternoon, because I know what giddiness is. I can remember the sensation I had, just as I can remember the colour I saw. I feel the same sensation, and that is the same colour. But the identity—the sameness—comes from the language.

A rule is something that is kept. The meaning of a word is something that is kept. It is for this reason that I can say this is the same colour I saw a moment ago. I can see the same colour just because I know red when I see it. And even with shades for which we have no special names, the same thing holds: I know the same colour when I see it.

It is similar, I have said, with sensations. I can say what I felt and I can say what I feel, and I can say it is the same sensation this time—because I know what sensations I am speaking of. It might be said that I can know it is the same only if it *feels* the same; and that is something no language can tell me. Nor can I know whether you are feeling the same as you have felt before. Only you can tell me that, because you are the only one who knows what it feels like. Well I agree that no language can tell me whether this feels the same. No language can tell me whether those two are the same colour, either. And my familiarity with methods of measurement will not tell me whether those two plots have the same area before I have measured them. But without language I could not have told whether this feels the same, either; if only because I could not have asked.

Of course recognizing a sensation is a different sort of thing from recognizing a colour. This holds whether I am speaking of my own or another's. It is different from recognizing what anything looks like or what is going on. When I say the dog is in pain I am not describing what the dog is doing, any more than I describe what I am doing when I give expression to pain. It is more like an expression of pity. At any rate, feeling pity, trying to ease him and so on—or perhaps turning away from the sight —is all part of believing that he is in pain. And to say that I was obviously justified in that—or maybe that I was mistaken—is a different sort of thing from saying that I was justified or mistaken in believing that he had a fracture. 'Mistake' means something different here, although it is just as definite. If I made a mistake in thinking the boy was in pain, well he was shamming and my pity was misplaced. The mistake was not that I supposed something was going on in him when nothing was. I may have supposed that too, perhaps that he had a cramp, but that is a different mistake. The dog's pain is not something going on. It is just his *being* in pain. I know for certain that he is in pain, and I know this because I know what pain is and what suffering is. There is an important difference between seeing that he is in pain and being in pain myself, because I do not see that I am in pain, and while it is conceivable that I am mistaken about him, that makes no sense in my own case. But this does not mean that I know something about myself which I cannot know about him.

We do not speak of sensations in the same way as we speak of processes or of colours. The name of a sensation is a different sort of name from the name of a colour. But if it means anything to say I am in pain again or that he is in pain again, this is because the word 'pain' has a regular use and because we know this when we know what pain is. If it were something I knew only in myself, then I might say 'This is something different now' or 'This is the same again' or I might say neither, and in any case it would not make any difference. This is not a question of whether I can trust my memory. It is a question of when it makes sense to speak of remembering; either of a good memory or a faulty one. If I thought I could not trust my memory, then of course I might look for confirmation. But there cannot be any question of confirmation here, nor any question of doubting either. There is just no rule for what is the same and what is not the same; there is no distinction between correct and incorrect; and it is for that reason that it does not make any difference what I say. Which means, of course, that I say nothing.

I cannot say anything unless I know the language. But I cannot know the language—any language—privately. I may have a secret code, but that is not the point here. It is a question of whether I can have a private understanding; whether I can understand something which *could* not be said in a language anyone else could understand. ('He may understand the language I speak, but he will not understand what I understand.') I say I cannot know a language privately, for what would there be to *know*? In language it makes a difference what you say. But how can it make any difference what you say privately? (I do not mean talking to yourself.) It seems that in a private language everything would have to be at once a statement and a definition. I suppose I may define a mark in any way I wish. And if every use of the mark is also a definition—if there is no way of discovering that I am wrong, in fact no sense in suggesting that I might be wrong—then it does not matter what mark I use or when I use it.

One might ask, 'Why can I not give myself a definition and decide for myself what following the definition is going to be?' But when? Each time? If I decide once and for all, that only renews the problem: what is 'according to my decision'? But what would the decision be anyway? In ordinary language I may decide to use an expression in a particular way, and I know how to keep to this. I do this in connexion with established usages and rules. That is why 'in a particular way' means something. That is also why I can decide to use the expressions of a secret language or the signs of a code in a particular way. For I am dealing with expressions that can be understood, and I know how the matter could be said in ordinary language. I know whether I am saying the same as I said before, and I know what I am deciding. But not when it is something which *could* not be said in ordinary language. Here there would be no point in saying, for instance, 'I am going to use S to mean that', because I do not know what 'meaning that' could be.

The reason is not that others must see what my words refer to. It is just that if my words are to refer to anything they must be understood. They cannot refer at all except in connexion with a use, a use which you learn when you learn what the word means. They cannot refer to anything unless there is a way in which the language is spoken. That is why there cannot be a private understanding. If it makes no difference what is said, nothing is understood.

There is of course no reason why I should not give an account of something which only I can see. Or of something which only I can feel: as when I tell a doctor what I feel in my abdomen. He does not feel my sensations (if that means anything), but he knows what I am talking about; he knows what sensations they are.

Ayer asks why Crusoe should not invent names for his sensations. (He actually says 'names to *describe* his sensations', but I do not understand this.) *I* can invent names for my sensations. But that is because I speak a language in which there are names for sensations. I know what the name of a sensation is. Inventing a name or giving it a name is something that belongs to the language as we speak it.

It is possible, certainly, to invent new expressions, and even in one sense new languages. But it is a different question whether anyone could have invented language. If language were a device or a method which people might adopt, then perhaps he could. But it is not that. And you could as easily speak of someone's inventing commerce; more easily, in fact. For he would have to invent what we call use and meaning. And I do not say so much that this would be beyond anyone's powers as rather that it is unintelligible.

The expressions of a language get their significance and their force from their application, from their extensive uses. Many of them enter in almost everything we do. And this gives them the force and obviousness they have in new contexts. So even if someone dreamed of a language before there was any, how could he put that forward as 'a practical proposition'? Or *what* would he put forward? Marks and sounds would be so much gibberish. To invent a vocabulary he would have at least to invent ways of using these sounds in various circumstances—in circumstances of a social life which has in fact grown up *with* language and could no more be invented than language could. And people would have to understand them. They would have to see not just that this sign occurs here and that there; they would have to see the difference it makes if you use the one or the other. And once again the difficulty is that there would be nothing to understand; because there would be no established use, and nothing we should call 'the difference it makes'.

Wittgenstein did not say that the ascription of meaning to a sign is something that needs justification. That would generally be as meaningless as it would if you said that language needs justification. What Wittgenstein did hold was that if a sign has meaning it can be used wrongly. On the other hand, if anyone had tried to invent language and teach it to others, then you might say the language and the use of expressions did stand in need of justification.

But why could not a dominant individual have brought people to behave as the people in one of Wittgenstein's primitive language games do? Why could he not force them to that as we train animals? Why could he not train them to respond in regular ways when ordered, and perhaps to answer?

Well, no animals have been trained to do even the primitive things that are done in those language games. Those people are not just going through a complicated trick; what they say depends upon what they need and what they find. They are not just carrying out orders. They use the expressions they do because they have something to say, and because that use is understood by all parties. Whereas although you may train animals to make the 'correct' responses to different words or signs, the animals themselves do not *use* different words. A dog may respond in one way to 'Slippers!' and in another way to 'Basket!', but he does not himself have one sound for the one and a different sound for the other; neither does he do anything like always giving two barks when he wants food and one bark when he wants a drink. No training has brought an animal to speak, even in a primitive way. This is not a question of the capacities of animals. If any animals do learn to speak, they will not learn it just as they learn tricks. A dog 'knows what you want him to do' when you utter the word, but he does not know what it means.

If people merely carried out orders and made certain utterances when they were ordered—if this were 'making the signs they were supposed to make when they were supposed to make them' —they would not be speaking. I suppose people might be trained to do that with Greek sentences without knowing Greek. And the people in our example would not understand what they were saying. They could not do that unless they used the expressions themselves, and using them is not just doing what you are told with them. What we call following a rule in language is not following orders. That is why we talk about 'taking part in' a language—the language is not any one man's doing more than another's and the rules, if they are rules of language, are not one man's rules. This is essential for understanding.

It might be that when people had been trained as we imagined they would eventually begin to speak. But that would not be what was invented, and it would not have come about by invention. It would have grown up through the initiative and spontaneous reactions of various people, none of whom was inventing language.

We might ask for *whom* would anyone invent language? Or for what? For animals, for instance? Or for people who have a social life as we have? If it is the latter, he need not trouble, for we have it. But unless it is for those who have the kind of social life people with languages do have—then what is the point and what is he inventing? What would a 'language' for a flock of parrots be, for instance? Can you get anywhere except by absurdly imagining them to live as human beings do, as in chilren's stories?

The point is that no one could invent just *language*. Language goes with a way of living. An invented language would be a wallpaper pattern; nothing more.

A man might invent marks to go with various objects. That is not language. And when Ayer's Crusoe invents *names* to *describe* flora and fauna, he is taking over more than he has invented. He is supposed to keep a diary, too. Ayer thinks that if he could do that when Friday was present he could surely have done it when he was still alone. But what would that be—keeping a diary? Not just making marks on paper, I suppose (or on a stone or what it might be). You might ask, 'Well what is it when *I* do it? And why should it not be the same for him, only a bit more primitive?' But it cannot be that. My marks are either marks I use in communication with other people, or they stand for expressions I use with other people. 'What difference does that make? He can *use* them just as I do.' No, because I use them in their various meanings. He cannot do that.

What is it he cannot do? What is it that I can do and he cannot? There seems to be nothing logically absurd in supposing that he behaves just as I do. To a large extent I agree. But it is absurd to suppose that the marks he uses mean anything; even if we might want to say that he goes through all the motions of meaning something by them.

I should agree that if 'meaning something' were something psychological, he might conceivably do that. If it were a question of what is put into my mind by my association with other people, then there is nothing logically absurd in supposing this to come into someone's mind without that association.

'What is it that I can do . . .?' To say that meaning something must be something *I* do is rather like saying it is something that happens at the moment. The point is that I speak a language that is spoken. What I say has significance in that language, not otherwise. Or in other words, if I *say* anything I must say it in some language. If there were no more than my behaviour, the marks I make and so on, then I should not mean anything either.

If I say there is 'more' than that—it is that I use the expressions in the meanings they have. If Crusoe used the same expressions he would not do that. Nor can he use different expressions but in these meanings. He does not use expressions in any meanings at all.

Using them in their meanings is what we call following a rule. For language there must be 'the way the expressions are used', and this goes with the way people live. I need not live that way myself when I use them. Defoe's Crusoe could have kept a diary, but Ayer's could not. Defoe's Crusoe's diary need never be read by anyone, and the meaning of what he writes does not depend on that. What he writes down may never play a part in the lives of other people. But the language in which he has written it does. And for that reason he can understand what he writes, he knows what he is saying. He knows the use or application of the expressions he uses, and it is from that they get the significance they have for him. He knows what he is talking about. Ayer's Crusoe does not and cannot.

Ayer's Crusoe may use marks for particular purposes—to show where he has hidden something, perhaps—and with as great regularity as we care to think. This is not what we mean by the regular use of an expression in a language. If he should suddenly do something which *we* should call using these marks entirely differently, it would have no sense to say that he had done anything wrong or anything inconsistent with what he had done before. We could not speak of his using them in the same meaning or in a different meaning. If he always uses them for the same purpose—as he might always gather wood for the same purpose—this is not what we mean by using an expression in the same way. *Using an expression in the same way does not mean using it for the same purpose.* (What I said about identity is connected with this.) And if there is any sort of discrepancy between what I said at one time and what I say at another—this does not mean that what I do with a mark or sound at one time is different from what I did with it before. If I have always done this with the mark, there is nothing of a rule of language in that.

'But if he uses them just *as* they would be used by someone who spoke the language, so that they *could* be understood, what is the trouble with saying that he uses them in their meanings?' The first trouble is that he does not understand them. And this really means that he does *not* use them just as someone who spoke the language would. For he cannot be guided by his signs in just the way in which you and I may be guided by words.

This is not a question of something beyond his powers. If we ask whether a machine could follow words, or whether a machine might speak, we are not asking what a machine might be designed to do. It is not a question of capacity or performance at all.

If you say something to me I understand you. If a tape recorder plays back what you have said, I understand what I hear but I do not understand the tape recorder. Which is a grammatical statement: I do not fail to understand either. If I say that you have said something but the tape recorder has not, I am not saying that something has happened in your case which did not happen in the other. But I do have an entirely different attitude towards you and towards what I hear from you, and I behave towards you in a host of ways as I should never behave towards a machine—for instance I may answer you, and I should never answer the recorder. I should not try to answer you either, nor should I suppose you had said anything, unless I assumed you knew the language; or unless I thought you said something in a language I did not understand. And I take it for granted you are speaking the language as it is spoken.

I am hardly ever in doubt whether you said something, if I have heard you. But I should begin to doubt if I found that you did not follow my answer, and that you did not seem to know anything about the matters to which your words referred. What I should be doubtful about, in that case, would not be whether something went on in you. I should be doubtful whether you knew what you were saying. But for all I know you may have 'done' all that you would have done if you had. The trouble is that your utterance was not a move you were making in the conversation or in the language at all.

If I doubt whether you know the language, or if I doubt

whether you ever know what you are saying, then in many ways I must regard you more as I should regard the tape recorder. This is not because you do not do anything that other people do. It is because you do not take part in what they do. You do not speak the language they speak. And *speaking* the language they speak is not just uttering the words; any more than understanding the language is just 'recognizing' the words. It is carrying on a conversation, for instance; or it may be writing reports, or listening to a play in a theatre. It is being someone to whom the rest of us can speak and get an answer; to whom we can tell something and with whom we can make a joke and whom we can deceive. All this, and of course immeasurably more, belongs to speaking the language. And it belongs to being able to follow words. You can follow words because you know how to speak. And for the same reason a machine cannot follow words. This has nothing to do with any question of what physics and engineering may achieve. It is just that it makes no sense to say that a machine might follow words.

One can say that absolutely of a machine, but not of Crusoe, because Crusoe might learn a language. But so long as he never has learned a language, in the sense of taking part in a language, it is as meaningless to say of him that he follows words as it would be to say this of an electronic computor.

I cannot ask whether a machine has made a mistake or whether it meant what it said. A machine may be out of order, and then you cannot rely on it. But it is not making a mistake. (And when I make a mistake myself there is nothing out of order.) A machine may 'correct mistakes' in connexion with the operation of negative feed-back. But there is nothing there like a mistake in understanding; nor like a mistake in calculation either. This is one reason why a machine cannot follow words—why that makes no sense. I can follow words only where a mistake or a misunderstanding is at least conceivable. ('Yes, of *course* that's what it means.') Otherwise there would be nothing like what we call understanding them.

I may react to words, rightly or wrongly, when I do not understand them. They may be words in a language I do not know, but I may have been taught to obey the orders of someone who shouts them. Maybe no one else would use them in these orders as he does, and that is of no consequence to me. It would have been exactly the same if he had used sounds of his own instead of words. I may react wrongly, as an animal might. But if I call this making a mistake, it is not like mistaking the meaning of the words he uses; any more than I have shown I understand the words if I make no mistake. I know what he wants, that is all. (I know enough to get out of the way of a barking dog, too.) If I had understood the words I should probably know what they would mean in other situations; and at any rate I should know what they would mean if somebody else used them too. The latter is the important point. It is connected with the fact that if I understand the words I should be able to use them, at least in some measure, myself. That is essential if I am guided by the words or if I follow them. But if that is necessary for understanding the words, it is also necessary for misunderstanding them; by which I mean again that it makes no sense to talk about misunderstanding apart from that. Misunderstanding or mistaking the meaning belongs to taking part in the language. You cannot speak of it otherwise.

Ayer's Crusoe may make the kind of mistakes animals do. He may mistake a bird which he does not like to eat for one which he likes. This is not like a mistake in understanding the meaning of an expression, or a mistake in following what was said.

'Why not? He calls the edible bird *ba*, and when he sees the inedible one he says "ba" and kills it.'

That is not a mistake in following the meanings of words. He could have made the same mistake without using words at all. (Perhaps it is roughly the kind of mistake that is corrected through negative feed-back.) You cannot ask whether he made the other kind of mistake; any more than you could ask this of a machine.*

I can mistake the meanings of the words you use, because I might use those words myself. If different people can use the same words, then the meanings are independent. I may also take your words in the wrong way. That is rather different, but it is connected with this. He said, 'I wonder how long it can last', and she thought he was finding their affair intolerable, whereas he meant the opposite. She knew the meanings of the

---

* Ayer says Crusoe may think that a bird is 'of the same type as one which he had previously named, when in fact it is of a different type, *sufficiently* different *for him to have* given it a different name if he had observed it more closely'. What do the words I have italicized mean here?

words he was using, and she could not have misunderstood him in that way unless she had. He might have used the same words to mean what she thought he meant. But he could not have meant either the one or the other unless his words had meant what they do independently; unless they had been the words of a language. I call their meanings 'independent', partly because they have to be learned. That is characteristic of language.

Unless the meanings of words were independent—unless they had to be learned—they could not be misunderstood. You do not misunderstand just a sound. You mistake the cry of an animal for the cry of a bird. You may mistake the call of an enemy for the call of a friend. That is not misunderstanding, not in the present sense. If one spoke of learning the meaning of a sound, that would not be like learning the meaning of a word. Perhaps it would not be nonsense to say that he 'knew instinctively' that it was the cry of an animal. But it is nonsense to say that he knew instinctively the meaning of a word.

You can misunderstand what you can learn. And you are misunderstanding a rule—not a matter of fact. Mistaking the cry of a bird for an animal cry is not misunderstanding a rule.

If one spoke of the independent existence of a tree, this might mean partly that I could think there was no tree there and be wrong. But the meanings of words are not quite comparable with that, and by their independence I do not mean quite the same. If I am wrong about the tree, I may run into it. If I am wrong about the meaning of a word, it is not like that. It is just that I use the word incorrectly, or understand it incorrectly. And that seems almost like saying that if I am wrong I am wrong. Which in a sense is just what I do mean. That is why it is better in this case to say that 'the meanings are independent' means just that they have to be learned; as a rule has to be learned. And that is why it is natural to speak of *misunderstanding* here; as it is not, so much, when you are speaking of a mistake in fact.

If anyone did not understand what kind of mistake it is, he would not understand the difference between correct and incorrect; and vice versa. But then he would not understand what words are.

. Now since you have learned the meanings of the expressions you use, it may happen that you do not mean what you say. At least it makes sense to ask of anyone who has spoken whether he meant it. If he does not mean what he says, this is familiar and definite enough, but you cannot describe it by describing what he is doing. You can describe it only by taking into account his relation to other people. In this case it is not simply that various people use the same words, although that is a large part of it. What is important is the special role or part played by the person in saying them. That is what his 'not meaning them' is. And it is as characteristic and essential for language as independent meanings are. I have said it is essential that different people may use the same words. But if those people were all doing the same thing, it would not be language. There must be something more like an organization, in which different people are, as we may put it, playing different roles. (The simile limps, but it has something important too. It must serve here.) That belongs to the use of language. Without it there would not be words and there would not be meaning.

Language is something that is spoken.

6

Wittgenstein's Builders

When Wittgenstein says that an account of what 'language' means would be something like explaining what 'game' means, he is not thinking of an explanation you would give to anyone in an ordinary way, but of the explanation you might give in philosophy. And then the trouble is to know what that is: what kind of explanation does one look for here? He gives an analogy when he refers to the explanation of 'game', but it is never more than an analogy, and at times we may feel unsure just how to take it. There is the analogy between speaking and playing a game too, of course. But I am thinking of the analogy in the idea of 'explanation': the analogy which should show what 'explaining what it means' or 'explaining what it is' may be.

Wittgenstein did not always distinguish between 'language' and 'speaking', and sometimes this brings trouble. Suppose you say that 'speaking' covers a family of related cases, just as 'game' does. And suppose you then say that language—or the language we speak—*is* a family of language games. Here you would not be saying simply that the games are various instances of what we call language; but that *a* language is a family of language games: that this is the kind of unity a language has. And this distinction is important, especially in connexion with the ideas of 'a common language' and 'something said in the same language'. I will return to this.

If we consider 'speaking', especially, there are certain ways in which the analogy with an explanation of 'game' is hard to use. I suppose you might try to tell someone what 'game' means by describing various games to him. (You must have come to the conclusion that he had never played one.) We could say then that he learns what 'game' means in this way, or that he has come to understand what a game is. But if you were trying to explain to someone what 'speaking' means, it could not go like that at all. If you think he has never even played a game, you begin by describing the various cases. But if you thought he had never learned to speak . . . you would not begin by describing how it goes.

He cannot understand what speaking is, unless he can understand what is said. And if he can understand what is said, what is the explanation supposed to do? (The question of how a foreigner learns the English word 'speaking' would not be relevant.)

'You may have played games often enough without ever having tried to say what playing a game is. And you may have spoken for years without ever having tried to say what speaking is.' But these cases are not really parallel. If you try to say what playing a game is, you try to show in a general way what people are doing when they play games: you describe examples enough to give an idea of it, and say 'and so on'. But although 'what people are doing when they play games' is all right here, a description of what people are doing when they speak would not do as an illustration of what speaking is.

Suppose I describe what the two men are doing while they are building, as Wittgenstein does in the *Investigations* (pp. 3 and 5). If this does illustrate speaking for you, then you must not only understand what they are doing, but you must understand what they say. My description must show that they speak a language which each of them understands, and which you also understand, if the illustration is to help you. (Wittgenstein imagines them using German words. He would say this was of no consequence, I think.)

If anyone says anything, he says it in a language. If he says anything he can speak with people, and for this they must speak a common language. I can understand what is said, or at least I can try to, if I speak the language.

This is one of the reasons why it is so hard to see clearly what 'a general account of language' would be. The difficulty is not simply in wondering whether 'Those are all examples of language' means that they must have some general features in common, since we use the same word. That would be the sort of thing we might ask about the generality of 'game'. The trouble is in this idea of 'the same language', when I say we speak the same language, for instance. As if the remarks that are made in the same language have something in common, so if you know the language you can understand them.

When Wittgenstein was writing the *Tractatus* he might have said that 'being in the language' meant simply being language or being a proposition. 'Die Gesammtheit der Sätze ist die Sprache.' And anything meant by a *common* language was covered, if at all, by this notion of being language or being intelligible. For he argued that all propositions must have a kind of common intelligibility or commensurability simply through being propositions or having sense.

That idea of 'all propositions' was extremely troublesome, and when Wittgenstein was writing the *Investigations* he had dropped it. The idea of 'belonging to language', like the idea of 'human language' (cf. 'ein bestimmtes Bild der menschlichen Sprache') was difficult too, though in different ways. But Wittgenstein has kept this. He is still interested in 'human language' rather than in the language or languages which people speak. When he says that any language is a family of language games, and that any of these might be a complete language by itself, he does not say whether people who might take part in several such games would be speaking the same language in each of them. In fact I find it hard to see how on this view they would *ever* be speaking a language. But these questions are complicated.

2

If I say something like 'I may know well enough what a game is and still be unable to *tell* you in any general way what a game is', I am thinking about the word and of certain difficulties one sometimes feels about it: the question perhaps of what guides people when they call one thing a game and another not, or perhaps of the kind of generality the word has. For there might be misunderstandings about this, even when no one had misunderstood the word. And if we could get clear on these questions, then at any rate we should have a better understanding of how we used it.

But if we were trying to get a better understanding of language it would be different. There are misunderstandings here and that is why we ask, but they are not like the misunderstandings people may have about their use of the word 'game'.

If you did say that our trouble is in finding a satisfactory account of the way the word 'language' is used, then I have tried to show that this trouble is peculiar, and it cannot be dealt with in the way the trouble about the word 'game' might.

The misunderstandings here are what Wittgenstein used to call 'misunderstandings of the logic of our language', which give rise to the problems of philosophy. I think the point is: one is perplexed as to whether something can be *said* or not. Or more commonly, what one is trying to say shows that one is confused about this. It is a confusion or uncertainty connected with being able to speak, and so perhaps with learning to speak: a confusion in connexion with what it is that one was learning as one learned to speak: with what saying something is and what understanding is. This sort of confusion or uncertainty (which is not just a confusion of the grammars of particular expressions) has led men to the scepticism which runs in one way or another into all the big questions of philosophy. And the understanding which philosophy seeks is in some sense an understanding of language or of what language is.

When Wittgenstein wrote the *Tractatus* he might have said that you understand the logic of language when you understand the syntax of a symbolism—or perhaps of *symbolism* as such. And in his later view he still would say that the logic of language is concerned with how words mean—which covers much of what he had meant by 'how signs symbolize'. But there is not the same idea of the *laws* of symbolism now, nor of the essential nature of signs. And he no longer thinks it important to find a symbolism which would show unambiguously the logical forms of the various statements; whereas in the *Tractatus* he thought that without this we cannot show their relations to reality. Unless we can find their logical forms we cannot find 'how they mean': we cannot understand what it is that makes them statements at all.

In the earlier view, then 'understanding the logic of language' and 'understanding the relation of logic to language' seem to coincide.

In the later view it is not so. He still says that 'we learn logic as we learn the language', but this is more important for what it tells you about logic than for what it tells you about language. But when we try to understand the logic of language, we are generally not concerned with the logical forms of statements, nor with the logical structure of language. In fact that idea of 'the logical structure of language' would illustrate what he would now call a *misunderstanding* of the logic of language. The whole idea of a structure or system, like the idea of a logical connexion, depends on what speaking is. But this is hardly even a statement, because speaking is not one thing, and 'having meaning' is not one thing either. This is perhaps the hardest thing to understand about language, and it is for this that he refers to the language games.

When he says that a child learns various language games as it learns to speak, he is thinking partly of how the parents teach the child to use the different expressions. But he is also explaining what 'teaching him expressions' *is*: what it is to be an expression or to mean something, and what it is to have a language. This is nothing that would help you in teaching a child and in one sense it says nothing about language: nothing that would interest philologists, for instance. But if you explain to me the various games, if you explain what we do with the various colour words, or how we use 'good' or 'continuity' or 'mind'— the games we play with them—you will have shown me how it is that they have meaning. In this way you will have shown me what makes it possible for language to have meaning, even though you have not referred to any general form or structure. You will have shown what it is for people to talk about things.

I think that is roughly Wittgenstein's position. But it takes for granted that it is the same language that is spoken in the various games. Much of what he says about the dangers in philosophy of being confused about the game we are playing when we talk about sensations and the game we are playing when we talk about physical objects, for instance, depends on that. And if we do say we are speaking the same language in the various games, then what does 'speaking the language' mean here? We cannot give an explanation of this by describing the game that is played.

It seems to me the trouble lies still in some unclarity about what the explanation is supposed to do.

3

It is especially difficult when Wittgenstein speaks as though we might regard the different language games as different languages. He speaks so in the beginning of the *Brown Book*, for instance, and in the early examples like that of the builders in the *Investigations* too. And the comparison of 'game' and 'language' fosters it, when this is meant to show what is meant by 'make up a family of cases'. For the 'cases' of games are all games themselves; and of course they do not *make up* a game. Different languages would not make up a language either. This shows that I am pushing the analogy in a way that it was not meant to go. And I admit I am puzzled. Suppose we say that we are playing a different language game when we are talking about our feelings and when we are talking about physical objects like motor-cars. Obviously these different language games are not different languages in the sense in which French and English are, because for one thing it would seem from some accounts as though people might be said to be playing the same language game either in French or in English, but more especially because it would make no sense to talk of translating from the one language game into the other. On the other hand, Wittgenstein did say in the *Brown Book*, for instance, that the various language games he had mentioned as making up a language were to be regarded 'not as incomplete parts of a language, but as languages complete in themselves, as complete systems of human communication' (p. 81). In this he is warning against the mistaken idea that a language may be found to be 'incomplete', and against a view like that of the *Tractatus* that it should be possible to calculate all the possible forms of proposition. There is a great deal in the philosophy of logic that is connected with that, and the criticisms Wittgenstein is developing in what he says about language games go deeper, probably, than any others have. But they also raise new issues themselves.

In the builders example in the *Investigations* Wittgenstein describes two men working with building stones. At various points in their work one of them shouts orders, for which he has a very limited number of expressions, and the other reacts to the orders by, for instance, bringing a slab when the first one shouts 'slab!' He then says that these men might have no other speech or language except this; and even that this might be the entire language of a tribe. It would be used, presumably, only in this kind of building work. But I feel there is something wrong here. The trouble is not to imagine a people with a language of such a limited vocabulary. The trouble is to imagine that they spoke the language only to give these special orders on this job and otherwise never spoke at all. I do not think it would be speaking a language.

When Wittgenstein suggests that in this tribe the children might be *taught* these shouts and how to react to them, I suppose this means that the adults would be using the expressions in giving the instruction, and this would be different from using them on the actual job. If they belong to a language, this is natural enough, just as it would be natural for the builders to use them in referring to the job when they had gone home. But then using the expressions and understanding the expressions would not be simply part of the building technique. Understanding 'slab' would not be just reacting correctly on the job.

If it is an actual building job, it will not always go according to plan; there will be snags. But when these builders come on a snag which holds up the work and baffles them, then although they have been speaking to one another in the course of their routine, they do not speak while they are trying to find what the trouble is. What they have learned are *signals* which cannot be used in any other way.

In fact it seems as though Wittgenstein has described a *game* with building stones, and not the sort of thing people would do if they were actually building a house. In a game there are no snags of the sort you meet on a job. And the signals are part of the game, too. But this will not do what Wittgenstein wanted. It does not show how speaking is related to the lives which people lead.

In any case—and this is my chief difficulty—if they had learned only those shouts and reactions there would not be any distinction of sense and nonsense. They might be nonplussed by a shout to which they had not been trained. But this would be no different from their bewilderment if someone moved a stone in a way that was not part of the routine in which they had been drilled.

Wittgenstein might say that for these people there would be no distinction between 'that is not what we generally do' and 'that makes no sense'. There might be some analogy to the example of the people who make no distinction between physical possibility and geometrical possibility (*Remarks on the Foundations of Mathematics*, p. 189). These people notice that when you fold a paper in this way, you get this sort of construction; and they never ask whether this is a geometrical relation of the figures, or whether it is a result of the physical properties of the paper. Similarly, the people in our present example would simply disallow or take no account of certain expressions; and it is pointless for us to ask whether they are rejecting them as nonsense or rejecting them because they are not part of the routine. (As we might take no notice of an utterance in some language which we did not understand.)

But I do not think this would be satisfactory. Unless there were a difference between learning to move stones in the ways people always do, and learning what makes sense, then I do not think we could say they were learning to speak.

Wittgenstein used to wonder whether there might be a people who had only an applied mathematics and no pure mathematics. Could we still say that they calculated and had proofs, although their proofs were something of the order of showing you what you can get if you fold the paper in this way: showing you what you will get if you use this method in numbering and separating sheep, and so on. These proofs would have nothing to do with 'concept formation', as the proofs of pure mathematics do. We might suppose the people used the proofs only for prediction: 'You can get it in this way.' The proofs would not then be normative, in the way the proofs of mathematics are. But just for this reason their whole position or role as proofs would become obscure. 'What puzzles me', Wittgenstein said, 'is how these proofs are *kept*.' They are a set of techniques which are used in forecasts, but they do not form a system in which there is any kind of dependence. And it is not clear how people would be persuaded to adopt them or what force they would have.

'That is just the way we do things.' Can we say that the sense or otherwise of what is said depends on that? Consider the question of whether he is using the words 'in the same way' for instance. What decides this? Or what does the question mean, even? In our language as we speak it there are standards of what is correct or incorrect, and these come in when we say he is not using the word in the same way now, or when we say someone has misunderstood. But I do not see how there can be any such standard in the game Wittgenstein has described.

In the *Remarks on the Foundations of Mathematics* (p. 133) Wittgenstein says, 'I want to say: it is essential to mathematics that its signs should also be used in civil life. It is their use outside mathematics, in other words the *meaning* of the signs, that makes the sign-game mathematics. Just as it is not a logical conclusion if I change one configuration into another (say one arrangement of chairs into another) unless these configurations have some use in language *besides* the making of these transformations.'

You might ask why this should make such a difference—the fact that they are used elsewhere. And one reason is that then the expressions are not just part of one particular routine. Their uses elsewhere have to do with the point or bearing of them in what we are saying now. It is the way in which we have come to know them in other connexions that decides whether it makes sense to put them together here, for instance: whether one can be substituted for another, whether they are incompatible and so forth. The meaning that they have within this game is not to be seen simply in what we do with them or how we react to them in this game.

The builders are not supposed to be drawing conclusions or calculating. But if they speak to one another, the meaning of the expression they use cannot lie wholly in the use or the reaction that it receives in this job. The point about the logical conclusion was that if the signs had no use or meaning outside this transformation, then the transformation itself would be without any significance and it would not show anything. If people are speaking together, then the significance of this or that remark is not like the significance of a logical conclusion. But the remarks they make have something to do with one another; otherwise they are not talking at all, even though they may be uttering sentences. And their remarks could have no bearing on one another unless the expressions they used were used in other connexions as well.

4

If someone learns to speak, he does not just learn to make sentences and utter them. Nor can he merely have learned to react to orders. If that were all he ever did, I should not imagine that he could speak, and I should never ask him anything. When he learns to speak, he learns to tell you something; and he tries to.

In learning to speak he learns what can be said; he learns, however fumblingly, what it makes sense to say. He comes to have some sense of how different remarks have something to do with one another. This is why he can answer you and ask you things, and why he begins to follow a conversation or to carry on a conversation himself. Or rather, it is misleading to say this is *why* he does that, as though what we had were a condition and

79

what results from it. For in beginning to carry on a conversation, in trying to tell you something and trying to understand your answer, he *is* getting a sense of how different remarks have a bearing on one another. And because he learns this, he can go on speaking or go on learning. If he can speak with me or ask me something here, then he will be able to ask me something else later.

By 'what it makes sense to say' I do not mean that he learns the correct way of using various expressions, although he does learn that. (He learns what pieces to call slabs and what to call beams, perhaps.) But 'what it makes sense to say' is not 'the sense these expressions have'. It has more to do with what it makes sense to answer or what it makes sense to ask, or what sense one remark may have in connexion with another.

He learns to tell you something. This is connected with the ideas of addressing you and greeting you. And you cannot teach it him by putting him through the motions.

Nor is it like learning a game. We may *use* something like a game in teaching him. We say his sounds back to him, and in this way we bring him to imitate other sounds we make. And this is a game. But it is not what we are trying to teach him. And if all he learns is how to play like this, he will not have learned to speak. He will never tell you anything nor ask you anything either.

When he can speak we may be delighted because 'He can say things himself now—not just repeat.' But what is important is that he can *say* things: not that he can construct new sentences —as it were in an exercise. You may set him exercises if you want to test his vocabulary. But this is not how you find out whether he can speak.

You might test his knowledge of a foreign language by setting him exercises too. And it would be something the same if you wanted to see whether he had mastered a particular notation. Or again, if you wanted to see whether he could do arithmetic. Wittgenstein used to speak of teaching a child to multiply by going through examples of multiplications for him, then getting him to go through these and through other exercises while you corrected his mistakes, and then saying 'Go on by yourself now.' But if you said anything similar about teaching a child to speak, you would have left out the most important thing. If he can speak, he has got something to tell you. In arithmetic it is different. Telling you things is not part of his achievement when he learns to multiply.

Learning to play a game is not just learning to do exercises either. And when Wittgenstein compared learning to speak with learning a game, one reason was that you generally play a game with other people. But this does not make it like conversation or like speaking. Not all speech is conversation, of course, but I do not think there would be speech or language without it. If there were someone who could not carry on a conversation, who had no idea of asking questions or making any comment, then I do not think we should say he could speak. Now one reason why a conversation is not like playing a game together is that the point of the various moves and counter-moves is within the game. Whereas we may learn from a conversation and from what is said in it. Generally each of us brings something to the conversation too: not as he might bring skill to the game, but just in having something to say.

I want to contrast (a) the external relations of the moves in a game, and (b) the internal relations of the remarks people make to one another. 'Internal relations' has a technical sense, so it may be misleading. But it does suggest 'connexions of meaning', and this is the point here. It cannot be reduced to connexions in a game. This goes with the fact that we can learn from a conversation: that its point is not contained just in what happens there.

And that is connected with the idea of having something to say. The point about chess, for instance, is that the pieces are furnished to you—you do not have to find them or decide what they shall be.

If you are giving me lessons in a foreign language, we may carry on a sham conversation to give me the opportunity of constructing appropriate sentences and giving appropriate replies. Neither of us learns anything from what is said in this, because neither of us really tells the other anything. And unless there were the distinction between genuine speaking and sham or pretence, then speaking *would* be nearly like playing a game.

Once more: if I know you can speak, then it makes sense for me to ask you what you mean, to try to get you to say more clearly what you want, and to ask you questions about it: just as truly as it makes sense for me to answer you. The example of the builders does not seem to allow for any of these. Neither could reply to the other—there is no such thing and it would have no sense. And there can be nothing of the sort so long as the meaning of the utterance is confined to 'what you do with it' in this particular connexion.

5

We are back at the question of what it is to have a language or what it is to speak. This is the question Wittgenstein is trying to answer in his analogy with games. He speaks of the games we play with this or that expression—with colour words, for instance, or with 'meter' or with 'good'. And one might ask, 'What is the objection to saying that the learning of these various expressions *is* learning to speak? There is not any *single* thing which is learning to speak—as though that were an operation too, or something over and above what we do with these various expressions. But knowing the use of such expressions—being able to use them on the occasions when they arise in connexion with other people—that is speaking.'

I could only answer what I have tried to say already. I do not want to suggest that there is some one thing which anyone learns when he learns to speak—especially if this means anything comparable to 'some one operation'. I have wanted to say that learning to speak is not learning *how* to speak or how to do anything. And it is not learning the mastery of a technique—although learning a foreign language might come nearer to that. (Not very near even then.) On the other hand, if it were really anything like what the paraphrase which I gave in the previous paragraph suggests—if that were all there were to it—then the child would not see the difference between a jumble of sentences and a sensible discourse. I have said that this is something that he learns, although it is not something you can teach him by any sort of drill, as you might perhaps teach him the names of objects. I think he gets it chiefly from the way in which the members of his family speak to him and answer him. In this way he gets an idea of how remarks may be connected, and of how what people say to one another makes sense. In any case, it is not like learning the meaning of this or that expression. And although he can go on speaking, this is not like going on with the use of any particular expression or set of expressions, although of course it includes that.

The remarks bear on one another. But not in the way in which parts of a technique do, nor as moves in a game might. If my remark has some bearing on yours, this is because of what I said and what you said: not just because our respective situations in this job have some bearing on one another too. This is why the remarks have to be understood before you can see what they have to do with one another—in a way that moves in a game do not.

If we ask *how* they are connected with other things that are said, for instance, we shall be raising questions I can hardly begin to discuss here. Wittgenstein used to say that to imagine a language is to imagine a form of life. This idea was important in his later writings, but he did not make very explicit what was included in it. Sometimes he speaks of it as a way of *working*, and it is hard to see the difference between this and a language game. Or he speaks of an institution like money, or an institution like buying and selling wood. But I think this is confusing. There is clearly some important connexion between the language a people speak and the life or culture they develop. And it is important to emphasize, as Wittgenstein was doing, that to understand what people are saying you must understand more than the vocabulary and the rules of grammar. But the differences between one form of life and another are not like the differences between one form of institution (say, marriage customs or financial institutions) and another. And the activity of the builders does not give you an idea of a people with a definite sort of life. Do they have songs and dances and festivals, and do they have legends and stories? Are they horrified by certain sorts of crimes, and do they expose people to public ridicule? The description of them on the building site, if you add 'this may be all', makes them look like marionettes. On the other hand, if they do have a life, then to say that their speaking is part of that life would be different from saying that their speaking is part of this activity of building.

Language is something that can have a literature. This is where it is so different from chess. And if we include folk songs and stories, then literature is immensely important in almost any language; important for the ways in which things said in the language are understood. It has to do with the 'force' which one remark or another may have in that language, for instance. And in this way it has to do also with what is seen to make sense and what is not.

Of course there is much else that is necessary as well. If you want to understand them you have to know what they are talking about. And for this you need to know how they farm and build and their marriage customs and the rest. I do not say this is less important than literature. I am saying only that it would be misleading to describe language as a part of that—as a part of the way or ways of doing things; especially if this leaves the suggestion that the language that belongs to building is no more closely connected with the language that belongs to the routine of a local government office, than are the movements they make in building and the movements they make in the office. Or that the language they use at home would have no other sort of connexion with the language they use at work than the way the home is run may have with the way the job is organized or the way the office is run.

The boy learns to speak so as to make sense and to find sense, and this is true in whatever job he happens to be or whatever he happens to be doing. In other words, there is a distinction between what we say and what we are talking about, and this goes with the idea of a reason for saying what we do.

This does not mean that the remarks made in the language form a system and that they get their sense from that. But it does suggest something like a common understanding. To think of language as a system, or as a kind of method (cf. 'a method of representation', 'method of projection'), almost as a kind of theory, is wrong if only because language is something people speak with one another. In this way it is not at all like mathematics. And it would be confusing to think that 'the language' is related to what is said in the language, as pure mathematics is related to applied mathematics. At the same time, the comparison does suggest something. And when I speak of a common understanding I do not mean simply what Wittgenstein used to call an 'agreement in reactions' which makes it possible to talk about using the word in the same way or using it correctly. It has to do rather with what is taken to make sense, or with what can be understood: with what it is possible to say to people: with what anyone who speaks the language might try to say.

7

'Unanswerable Questions'*

Although Bambrough discusses only three or four sorts of question, he thinks these are typical, so that what he says of them can be extended to all questions. But I do not understand this sense of 'all'.

If he had taken two or three typical questions in kinetics in order to bring out some general feature of questions in this field —or perhaps some illustrations of the kind of questions that belong to the study of history, or some typical questions in medical diagnosis—I could see the sense of speaking of all or most questions in this particular field. But would it have sense to say 'These are typical of all *questions*'? I do not see what 'typical' would mean.

There are questions or problems in mathematics, but what I might call typical of these would not be typical of questions outside mathematics. And what might be typical of questions asked in the course of preparing the annual accounts of a business would not be typical of questions asked in interviewing a candidate for a teaching post, nor of the questions a curious neighbour may ask the housewife who has just moved in, nor of the questions of a disappointed child.

Asking a question in one connexion may not be what it is in another. I do not mean, for instance, that you have to know something about a subject before you can know what questions to ask in it. (I cannot ask questions about football if I know nothing about the game and never follow it.) I mean that *asking* a question—as opposed to asserting or explaining or contradicting, etc.—is different in mathematics and in medicine; and different again in a family quarrel or in examining one's conscience.

If asking is different, answering will be; and also the sense of

* From a symposium with Renford Bambrough, 1966.

'are there unanswerable questions?' In certain cases it may have none. If we call *problems* questions (not always the other way round, for plenty of questions are not problems) then 'decision problems' in mathematical logic might be an example. If anyone said 'there are no unsolvable decision problems' no one would know what he meant. That there is sometimes a proof that the problem is unsolvable, belongs with the *meaning* of 'decision problem'. Bambrough might say these are technical senses of 'problem' and of 'solving', outside the limits of his thesis. But there are examples which are not technical and do not fall within his thesis either, as far as I can see.

I

Sartre's pupil will solve his moral problem if he can come to a decision. This is why no one can solve his problem for him. If I have got lost in a problem of statistics I may ask an expert to do it for me. He may explain the reasons for the way he goes about it, and why what I did was wrong. Sartre's pupil may be trying to find some reasons that will make it clear what he must do. But whatever the role of reasons here, they are never conclusive in the way the steps of a mathematical proof are, nor in the way in which material evidence of guilt may be. And further: what makes any circumstance or consideration a 'reason' for a decision? what makes it something that weighs in favour or weighs against deciding this way? What counts as a reason in my decision, might not have weighed with you in my position. So that the *problem* is generally not the same for one person and another.

But moral problems are a mixed bag. (People are vague about what it includes, and some can only stare in wonder at the examples others call typical.) In some of them reasons are recognized in other ways and have other functions than they had, I imagine, for the man Sartre tells of.

I might be wondering whether I ought to join the army, or whether I ought to join the Communist Party, or whether I ought to join the Church. These are serious steps, and I may ask another's advice—especially if I keep wondering whether 'in consistency' or 'if I am to be true to the principles I recognize' I ought to act in this way or in that. He may discuss with me what it is that such principles require, and whether they really require the actions I imagined they did.

It is different when a woman is wondering whether to leave her lover and return to her husband whom she does not love (like Sue in Hardy's *Jude the Obscure*); or a man must decide between staying with his wife and going to pieces, or leaving her and bringing disaster that way. Here it is not a question of what you ought in consistency to do.

I may be making a mistake in deciding to join the Communist Party, or in deciding not to. But we cannot speak of mistakes like this in the other case. I may feel it was a terrible thing for Sue to have taken the course she did (though if I do I have not understood much). But I could not say she missed the right decision and took the wrong one. If I tell you I am in agreement with all the main tenets of communism and I do not see how I can with any honesty stand back and refuse to join the Party— then you may question my conclusion. But there is nothing of this in Sue's problem. Her lover might say to her what Jude said; that is all. It would make no sense to ask which of them was right.

Her problem is not of seeing what it is she wants, but what she can do. Just what this perplexity is, is nothing another person can grasp or do much to imagine. It is with her that things weigh as they do; and however deeply you respect and try to understand her difficulty, it is never a difficulty you *have*. She is not trying to find the right answer. If you suppose she is . . . you cannot see the importance of the problem in her life, or how it can bring tragedy.

2

If Sartre claims that it would have no sense to say the man must *find* the right answer to his moral problems, he makes this plausible, Bambrough thinks, because he has taken a borderline case or a borderline question—comparable to the question 'Is this man bald?' He thinks 'the difficulty about borderline cases' is 'a feature of difficult moral dilemmas'. But I do not see the analogy between 'What ought I to do here?' and 'Is this man bald?' If the question about baldness is borderline, I do not think the other is.

In this example 'Is he bald?' is not a question of fact. Of course I might have asked it about someone I had never seen, and then it would be. But here I am not asking you to tell me anything about him; I am asking whether 'bald' is the word you would use here. And if you feel like shrugging your shoulders, this is not because you would have to examine the man more carefully before you could say. As far as that goes I can see him as plain as you can.

But in 'What ought I to do here?' the man is not undecided about the use of a word—as though he were not asking what to *do* but what to *call* the action before and after performing it. Bambrough thinks the trouble is in knowing where to place this problem among others which resemble it in different ways, and which are clearly *not* unanswerable. The man does not see in what respects his problem is like that other case, and where it is no longer like that and looks like *this* other case which he would answer in the opposite way. So the problem seems to have two faces—or rather to fluctuate from this face to that without showing any of its own. But if this is a difficulty, it is not what Sartre was talking about. As though the man were saying: 'When I see how much this is like a question of that sort, I say "yes, I must go"; but when I see how much it is like a question of this other sort, I say "no, I must not go". But . . . it is not definitely of the one sort or of the other, so I cannot say either "yes" or "no".' That would not be a moral difficulty—a difficult choice —at all.

What makes a moral decision difficult is not that I am bewildered by the rules or uncertain which rule applies here. It is that what I have to do goes against what I feel to be deeply important; I shall be doing what I feel I would give my life to *avoid* doing—harming those I least want to harm. The problem is difficult because *whichever* course I take I shall be doing something for which I can never forgive myself.

In any case, when I notice a resemblance between this problem and those others, and when I judge the degree and the importance of this resemblance, I am making judgments of value —choosing a frame of reference—whose character will depend on the moral convictions and moral feelings I have developed. Bambrough speaks of 'similarity' in this connexion almost as though it were like matching colours. He speaks of knowing 'where the case lies on the manifold of actual and possible cases', but he says nothing of how we decide on the *order* of cases in this manifold. If I say the resemblance to that problem is more important than the resemblance to this one—what sort of measure is this? If Bambrough says people never disagree in such judgments unless they are madmen or philosophers, he is making the circle of the brethren very wide.

When 'Is he bald?' is a borderline question I have no answer: but not because I waver between thinking how like he is to someone obviously bald, and how like someone who is not. Here Bambrough would agree. But why does he say that 'the case about which we ask ... has its own place in the manifold of cases ... the *continuum* of possible intermediate cases'? ('Case' is confusing here. Is it the state of the man's scalp? Or is it the grammatical form of question and answer?)

The point in speaking of a *continuum* of cases is to suggest that the 'cases' do not overlap: for if they did we could not say 'this case has just *that* place on the *continuum*, while *this* case has just *that* place', etc. And Bambrough does want to speak in this way.

I might make a film, or perhaps an animated cartoon, showing someone gradually growing bald: a thick head of hair growing steadily thinner on top, gradually leaving a bald spot and the bald area steadily spreading. We could draw sharp lines at various points in this film, but these would not correspond to our use of 'thick hair', 'slightly bald', 'quite bald', etc. For these are not expressions which vaguely indicate areas that fit end to end in a continuous transition. There could be no experiment to find just where the condition of not being bald ends and the condition of beginning to grow bald begins; where beginning to grow bald ends and 'being somewhat bald' begins, etc. What we speak of as 'beginning to grow bald' does not *have* an end, in that sense, nor a beginning either.

When Bambrough speaks, for instance, of 'the *midpoint* of the line' representing 'the *continuum* of possible intermediate cases', he seems to be thinking of a definite boundary distinguishing what is borderline from what is not. But this would mean nothing. No more than it would if we were using an expression such as 'roughly', 'somewhere about', 'near enough' —e.g., 'This stick isn't exactly three feet long.' 'Well, it's near enough'—and you wanted to determine the point where near-enough ends, and not-near-enough begins. (Wittgenstein would have said 'we are not speaking in that geometry'. Cf. *Philosophische Bemerkungen*, pp. 263ff.)

Suppose I show the film to someone slowly and stopping frequently to ask 'Is that beginning to go bald?', 'Is that partly bald?' and so on. When I have stopped I sometimes start again from a point a little further back. At one point the subject says, 'No, he is not yet beginning to go bald', and then when I show him what is in fact an earlier stage he says 'Yes, now he is'. There would be no reason to say either answer was wrong. Still less, as Bambrough suggests, that both were 'definitely wrong'. (I might have said 'as you like'—i.e., there is no objection to either, and no reason to prefer either. Of course, this does not mean 'it depends on whether you like it or not'.)

Obviously it would be nonsense to say that the top of his head is in an indeterminate state. And if we are puzzled by our use of the word 'bald', this is because we mix up describing the grammar of the word with what we describe when we use the word.

There is no definite answer to 'How much sand does there have to be to make a heap?' (Cf. Wittgenstein, loc. cit.) But we cannot say 'a heap of sand is something indeterminate'. It is just as determinate as a mountain is. If the question 'Is it a heap *now*?' leads sometimes to apparently contradictory answers although we would not say either was wrong, we do not conclude that we are dealing with a physical object which may have contradictory properties.

We do not use the *word* 'heap' or the expression 'heap of sand' as we use 'cord of wood' for instance. But this does not mean that a heap of sand is 'something of a different category' from a cord of wood.

It is important to emphasize that there *are* expressions of this sort—for which sometimes the question 'Is *this* one?' is undecided; and emphasize that this is a property of the expressions we are using. We may imagine a use of the expression 'number' with similar properties. If we say that in *this* use of 'number' there is no law of excluded middle, we are not calling attention to a special property of certain numbers—understanding the word now in the sense or senses generally recognized.

3

Bambrough says that 'the language of spatial location . . . may be extended in such a way as to provide a useful analogy for *logical* space, and hence for the whole nature of reasoning and classification'.

But he has made the extension the opposite way. He thinks of spatial location in analogy with position in logical space; and he has little to say about the kinds of reasoning that go with locating bodies in space.

I suppose he takes 'logical space' as the expression is used in the *Tractatus*—where a place in logical space is like a place in a system of co-ordinates, i.e., a *geometrical* place. This is the sense of *Tractatus* 3.4 and the three remarks which follow it. In 3.0321 Wittgenstein had emphasized the distinction between what is geometrically possible and what is physically possible. An occurrence is physically possible if, according to the observations we have made, its occurrence would be consistent with established laws of physics. The question 'Where is that body now?' would generally mean 'Which among the positions it *might* be in now ... ', i.e., positions *physically* possible for it, not just geometrically possible. Obviously the '*now*' is important, but so are other physical data.

In geometry the question 'where?' is like other questions in mathematics. 'Where is the highest point in this curve?' asks you to calculate or construct the highest point in the curve. (Cf. *Philosophische Bemerkungen*, p. 209.) There would be no difference between explaining or describing the construction and carrying it out. Or we might say roughly that in geometry there is no difference between explaining how to find the point and finding it. To ask 'Where is the highest point of the arch of this door-way?' would be another sort of question, and the answer would not make sense in geometry.

I should think it nonsense to say that 'something can exist in' a geometrical place—I should wonder what sort of 'can' that is, for one thing—although of course co-ordinate geometry is an important part of the *phraseology* in which we speak of the place of a physical body.

In most physics, I should have thought, the question 'Where is such-and-such a body?' would have no sense unless we knew the methods of measurement assumed by the person who asked it. These go with the *meaning* of 'the place where the body is'. We may say if we like that to understand the question we must know the methods to be used in finding an answer. But here of course explaining in detail how to carry out the measurements would not be the same as carrying them out.

Bambrough seems to confuse two questions:

(1) What do we regard as the marks which define a particular place?

(2) How do we decide whether a body is in that place or in some other?

He says that 'if I ask you where something is in space, you can answer my question only by referring to the position of something else in space'. This suggests that 'where is it?' can be answered always in the same way: that 'giving the place or the position' has always the same sense. But think of the phrase 'the position of a moving body at a particular time', for instance.*

Bambrough says nothing about alternative frames of reference in describing the positions and movements of bodies. But neither does he speak of the 'procedures for determining the location of an object' when we have *conflicting* answers to the question 'where?' I give a statement of where Land's End is that conflicts with your statement. Or you say the train is at that point now, and I say it is somewhere else. If we try to decide this, then part of what we do will probably be to *look and see* where certain things are (perhaps not the object in question, but others whose positions we must know if we are to say where that is). And here 'where they are' does not refer to the position of something else in space.

Suppose you are pointing to the ash tree because you want to tell me where you left the mower: 'A little to the right of that tree and ten yards further on.' I am looking at the tree to which you are pointing and I say 'But where is that tree?' Why is this nonsensical?

You might say 'Why it's right there where you see it.' But then you are not saying where it is in relation to anything else.

When I go to work some men from the Gas Board are trying to find where the leak in the gas main is. I come back during their dinner hour and I ask 'Well, where was it?' They take me along to show me. 'It was just *there*.' Is there anything relative about this?

I know what it means for a tree or a rock to be 'there' or 'here'. These are primitive starting points for our ideas of 'being somewhere'—the difference between being in one place and being in another—making it possible for concepts of location to come into what we say and ask about things.

I should think it obvious that they are prior to saying where something is by referring to the position of something else. If

* See below, p. 152.

Bambrough wants to say that I am introducing a different sense of 'where'—he will have gone far to agree with me.

When Bambrough speaks of positions, he is generally thinking of maps and geography: what we might call 'the relations of different *places* to one another'. But this leaves out a great deal. I may ask whether a particular road or river is where this map says it is—whether it is further from the coast than that pond is, etc. But this is not like trying to determine the position of a body which is sometimes in one place, sometimes in another. If I were misled about this, it would not be a mistake in geography.

'I know the river runs near to the north side of the church and the railway is to the south of it. So that church cannot be where the map says it is.' Would this be an example of those reasonings about location which Bambrough thinks 'well fitted to illustrate points about the nature of rational enquiry in general and as such'? It would be in line with his suggestion that you have settled the moral problem (or any other problem) when you 'know where the case lies on the manifold of actual and possible cases'.

But even if this 'manifold of cases' were something more than a vague image—even if we had any idea how the manifold was ordered, for instance—finding the 'place' of this moral problem among others will no more *solve* the problem than knowing the distances and directions of various places from one another will tell you where the motor-car is. Bambrough says of Sartre's example: 'Only because it is like so many that are clearly to be answered in one way, and also like so many others that are clearly to be answered in the opposite way, is it so well fitted for its role of sceptical conundrum.' But this does nothing at all to show that there must be a clear answer in *this* case. The contrary, if anything. And Bambrough entirely evades the question *whether there is a right solution to the problem* with which the man is faced. It is no *solution* to tell him that the two obligations are of equal weight—even if this *states* the problem more clearly.

Bambrough is misled by his own remarks about 'answers' in 'borderline cases'—where the question is whether to use this expression or not: a question about the use of words, not of how to find something or of what to do.

8

Some Developments in Wittgenstein's View of Ethics

In the *Tractatus* (6.42) Wittgenstein says 'there can be no ethical propositions', but he still thinks that speaking of good and evil means something. He has just said that 'in the world everything is as it is, and things happen as they do; *in* the world there is no value—and if there were any, it would have no value'. (Instead of 'a value that has value' he might have said 'that has value in itself' or 'absolute value'.) What there is, the kinds of things there are, and the ways in which things happen might have been otherwise: there is nothing special about their being as they are. He might have said that an expression like 'a value which has value' is nonsense born of a confusion of grammar, which a logical analysis would replace by something else. Instead he says that 'if there is a value which has any value, it must lie outside the whole sphere of what happens'. And it is because of what judgments of good and evil do mean that it is pointless to look for their meaning in any events or facts that might be found by science. 'There are no distinctions of absolute value' does not mean 'the phrase "distinctions of absolute value" means nothing'.

'There are no ethical propositions' was a commentary to 6.4: 'All propositions are of equal value.' This means first that all *logical* propositions are of equal value. No one logical principle and no special set of logical principles is the fundamental one and source of all the rest. None occupies an 'exceptional position'. But when he turns 6.4 towards 'ethical propositions' he does not refer to the equal value of all logical propositions but to that of all statements of fact. Perhaps no one would take an ethical judgment for the assertion of a logical principle, but one might think it some kind of description of what has happened.

Here again Wittgenstein is guided by what we do mean in these judgments.

Compare 'absolute value lies outside the world of facts' and 'logical necessity lies outside the world of facts'. Neither can be expressed, but logical necessity can be shown as absolute value cannot. We may show the necessity of logical principles by writing tautologies and contradictions in the T-F notation. The T-F notation is a logical symbol, not an explanation, and it is one in which we may write any other form of proposition as well. It is a notation in which they are shown to *be* propositions. It shows both how logical principles are distinguished from other propositions and how they are related to the form of proposition—to what it is to be a proposition at all. But the T-F notation is no help in ethical judgments; for where there is a judgment of absolute value, the question 'Is it true or false?' means nothing.

If I could express an ethical judgment, you might deny it, and of course it would mean nothing to say we were both right. But in the *Tractatus*, and in much of the *Lecture on Ethics*, Wittgenstein thinks of 'true or false' in the sense in which a prediction in science may be shown to be true or false. It would make no sense to ask if a judgment of absolute value had been corroborated by something that happened or something that had been discovered. We cannot ask this of logical principles either; but the T-F notation takes account of this, and it serves for logical principles because these are (as he later called them) rules of grammar of propositions which do allow of corroboration or falsification.

The explanation (of the difference between logical necessity and absolute value) by reference to the T-F notation is probably too simple. There are ethical statements, but they are expressed no differently from statements of fact; the ethical character is not shown in the symbolism. If we consider (6.422) an ethical law of the form 'You ought . . .' the first thought is, 'And what if I don't?'—as though it were a statement of *relative* value. With a judgment of absolute value the question makes no sense. But we might almost ask: 'By what logic?'

If I say, 'then the angles *must* be equal', there is no alternative; that is, 'the alternative' means nothing. If I say, 'You *ought* to want to behave better', there is no alternative either. The other may think, 'What if I don't?' if only because in fact

95

he does not and there is nothing to make him. Or he may be denying what I said: it may be a way of saying, 'There is no "ought" about it.' But if he means it as a question, he has mistaken what I said: he can ask it only because he thinks I meant something else.

'You ought to make sure that the strip is firmly clamped before you start drilling.' 'What if I don't?' When I tell you what will happen if you don't, you see what I mean.

But: 'You ought to want to behave better.' 'What if I don't?' What more could I tell you?

Yet 'There *is* no alternative' does not mean what it does in logic. 'If the legs of the triangle are equal, the base angles *must* be equal.' Suppose my first thought were: 'What if I make one with the legs perfectly equal and the base angles are not equal?' You say, 'Don't talk nonsense'; or you get me to look more closely at what I was trying to ask, and I say, 'Oh, yes.' When the man asked, 'What if I don't?' the question made no sense in that connexion, although it would in others. But when I tried to ask about the logical conclusion, it was not a question at all. (I do not think 'indirect proofs' make any difference here.)

We express (or try to express) judgments of value, not just any time, but in circumstances in which it makes sense to do so. Then there are certain replies one can make and certain questions one can ask, and others which would mean nothing. This is implied, at least, in the *Tractatus*. It is not worked out, and it hardly could be, with the views he then held about language and about sense.

He had changed them by the time of the *Lecture on Ethics*. He did not think one could give a general account of propositions in terms of truth functions. Every proposition belongs to some system of propositions, and there are a number of these systems. The formal rules or internal relations of one system are not those of another. He spoke of them as 'systems of measurement' and as 'independent co-ordinates of description'. Several will come into the description of one and the same state of affairs: the description is determined by several co-ordinates. He could not speak in this sense of a system of ethical propositions or judgments of value, as though we might determine the object's value along with its weight and temperature. And he still thought of language primarily as description. But the

'Lecture on Ethics' starts from examples more than the *Tractatus* does.

For instance, when someone says, 'I know I'm playing tennis badly, but I don't want to play any better', all the other man could say would be, 'Ah, then, that's all right.' He is making a judgment of value—not telling anyone what he has seen. And the 'could' expresses a rule of grammar. Then, when someone says, 'I know I behave badly, but then I don't want to behave any better', Wittgenstein asks whether you could make the same reply here, and answers 'certainly not', meaning that such a reply would make no sense. This has nothing to do with what would be intelligible in a description of facts. It is a question of what is intelligible in this game of ethical judgments. Towards the end of the lecture he does show how in our expressions of value judgments we may take a familiar word like 'safe' and join it with 'absolutely'—which is a distortion or a destruction of its meaning. But the example by which he first showed what he meant by a judgment of absolute value—'Well, you *ought* to want to behave better'—is a natural remark to make in the circumstances; the only remark you *could* make, in fact. It is not a distortion or misuse of language.

He says in the later examples that he would reject any analysis which showed that they were not nonsense—that they describe such and such experiences—because in those expressions he wishes to 'go beyond the world . . . that is to say, beyond significant language'. I think this goes with a view of judgments of value as expressions of will.

The *Tractatus* distinguishes the will that is good or evil from the will of which I have experience (this is a grammatical distinction). He had written in the *Notebooks* (p. 87) that 'the will is a position the subject adopts towards the world' (or he might have said, 'towards life'). I know only that 'I *have* to go that way'. I cannot do certain things without feeling ashamed. This is part of how I look on life, what I recognize that I must meet. In the same way, I may find problems where another would find none—or it may be the other way about. I praise the character a man has just shown, or I tell him 'You ought to want to behave better.' This refers to what he did or said here just now. But I am claiming that the significance of what he did 'goes beyond' these circumstances. A little earlier in the *Notebooks* (p. 83) he said that 'a good life is the world seen *sub specie*

97

aeternitatis. . . . . The ordinary way of looking at things sees objects so to speak from within their midst, the view *sub specie aeternitatis* from outside. So that they have the whole world as their background.' I suppose he disliked this phrasing, and the *Tractatus* phrasing is different. It may still do something to show why he separates judgments of value from statements of fact, and what he means when he says they cannot be expressed.

He criticized remarks of this sort later. If you have said what it is that cannot be expressed, we begin to wonder how expressing it would differ from saying what it is. Of course I may say, 'There is no one sentence which could convey all I meant when I thanked him.' To understand any judgment of value we have to know something of the culture, perhaps the religion, within which it is made, as well as the particular circumstances that called it forth; what the man had done, what the question was when I spoke to him, and so on. But suppose I have explained all this, we might still ask whether I have said something which has, for me and for some who heard me, a significance which 'goes beyond' all circumstances. What would it mean if I said it did have a significance of that kind? One answer is: that it goes deep with me when I say it; that it is anything but a *trivial* remark. This will appear especially in the way I behave after I have spoken: my behaviour towards the man I addressed and towards the one he wronged, for instance. (Here again: it has to be an occasion on which a remark *could* have that significance. To behave in this way otherwise would be ridiculous and annoying.)

If you said that the moral rebuke, if it is justified, has a significance beyond any circumstances, many would understand you. And if we describe the difference it makes when the remark is of this kind, we shall know what is meant by describing it as 'going beyond'.

The *Tractatus* is unclear in this because it does not mention the occasions or the problems in connexion with which a man might make such a judgment. We are not *always* viewing actions as we do in a judgment of value. The *Tractatus* speaks of 'problems of life'. But it does not ask—as Wittgenstein later did—*when*, or in what circumstances anyone would speak about problems of life.

Once (in 1942) when I had asked something about the study of ethics, Wittgenstein said it was strange that you could find books on ethics in which there was no mention of a genuine ethical or moral problem. He wanted to speak of a problem only where you could imagine or recognize a solution, I think. When I suggested the question whether Brutus's stabbing Caesar was a noble action (as Plutarch thought) or a particularly evil one (as Dante thought), Wittgenstein said this was not even something you could discuss. 'You would not know for your life what went on in his mind before he decided to kill Caesar. What would he have had to feel in order that you should say that killing his friend was noble?'* Wittgenstein mentioned the question of one of Kierkegaard's essays: 'Has a man a right to let himself be put to death for the truth?' and he said, 'For me this is not even a problem. I don't know what it would be *like* to let oneself be put to death for the truth. I don't know how such a man would have to feel, what state of mind he would be in, and so forth. This may reach a point at which the whole problem wavers and ceases to be a problem at all. Like asking which of two sticks is the longer when they are seen through the "shimmer" of air rising from a hot pavement. You say, "But surely one of them *must* be longer." How are we to understand this?' I suggested the problem facing a man who has come to the conclusion that he must either leave his wife or abandon his work of cancer research. 'Thanks,' said Wittgenstein, 'let's discuss this.

'Such a man's attitude will vary at different times. Suppose I am his friend, and I say to him, "Look, you've taken this girl out of her home, and now, by God, you've got to stick to her." This would be called taking up an ethical attitude. He may reply, "But what of suffering humanity? how can I abandon my research?" In saying this he may be making it easy for himself: he wants to carry on that work anyway. (I may have reminded him that there are others who can carry it on if he gives up.) And he may be inclined to view the effect on his wife relatively easily: "It probably won't be fatal for her. She'll get over it, probably marry again", and so on. On the other hand it may not be this way. It may be that he has a deep love for her. And yet he may think that if he were to give up his work he would be no husband for her. That is his life, and if he gives that up he will drag her down. Here we may say that we have all the materials of a tragedy; and we could only say: "Well, God help you."

---

* I am quoting from what I wrote down a few hours after the conversation. The quotation marks mean no more than that.

'Whatever he finally does, the way things then turn out may affect his attitude. He may say, "Well, thank God I left her; it was better all around." Or maybe, "Thank God I stuck to her." Or he may not be able to say "thank God" at all, but just the opposite.

'I want to say that this is the solution of an ethical problem.

'Or rather: it is so with regard to the man who does not have an ethics. If he has, say, the Christian ethics, then he may say it is absolutely clear: he has got to stick to her come what may. And then his problem is different. It is: how to make the best of this situation, what he should do in order to be a decent husband in these greatly altered circumstances, and so forth. The question "Should I leave her or not?" is not a problem here.

'Someone might ask whether the treatment of such a question in Christian ethics is *right* or not. I want to say that this question does not make sense. The man who asks it might say: "Suppose I view his problem with a different ethics—perhaps Nietzsche's —and I say: 'No, it is not clear that he must stick to her; on the contrary, . . . and so forth.' Surely one of the two answers must be the right one. It must be possible to decide which of them is right and which is wrong."

'But we do not know what this decision would be like—how it would be determined, what sort of criteria would be used, and so on. Compare saying that it must be possible to decide which of two standards of accuracy is the right one. We do not even know what a person who asks this question is after.'

He came back to this question of 'the right ethics' later. He did so once (in 1945) when he was discussing the relations of ethics and psychology and sociology. 'People have had the notion of an ethical theory—the idea of finding the true nature of goodness or of duty. Plato wanted to do this—to set ethical enquiry in the direction of finding the true nature of goodness— so as to achieve objectivity and avoid relativity. He thought relativity must be avoided at all costs, since it would destroy the *imperative* in morality.

'Suppose you simply described the *Sitten und Gebräuche* (ways and customs) of various tribes: this would not be ethics. Studying ways and customs would not be the same as studying rules or laws. A rule is neither a command—because there is no one who gives the command—nor is it an empirical statement of how the majority of people behave. Both those interpretations ignore the different grammars, the different ways in which rules are used. They are not used as commands are and they are not used as sociological descriptions are. If I buy a game in Woolworth's, I may find on the inside cover a set of rules beginning: "First set out the pieces in such and such a way". Is this an order? Is it a description—an assertion that anybody ever has acted or ever will act in that way?

'Someone may say, "There is still the difference between truth and falsity. Any ethical judgment in whatever system may be true or false." Remember that "p is true" means simply "p". If I say: "Although I believe that so and so is good, I may be wrong": this says no more than that what I assert may be denied.

'Or suppose someone says, "One of the ethical systems must be the right one—or nearer to the right one." Well, suppose I say Christian ethics is the right one. Then I am making a judgment of value. It amounts to *adopting* Christian ethics. It is not like saying that one of these physical theories must be the right one. The way in which some reality corresponds—or conflicts—with a physical theory has no counterpart here.

'If you say there are various systems of ethics you are not saying they are all equally right. That means nothing. Just as it would have no meaning to say that each was right from his own standpoint. That could only mean that each judges as he does.'

These samples (perhaps not well chosen) from his later discussions show parallels with his later discussions of language and of logic and mathematics. There is no one system in which you can study in its purity and its essence what ethics is. We use the term 'ethics' for a variety of systems, and for philosophy this variety is important. Obviously different ethical systems have points in common. There must be grounds for saying that people who follow a particular system are making ethical judgments: that they regard this or that as good, and so forth. But it does not follow that what those people say must be an expression of something more ultimate. He used to say that what we might call 'the anthropological method' had proved particularly fruitful in philosophy: that is, imagining 'a tribe among whom it is carried on in this way: . . . ' And once when I mentioned Goering's '*Recht ist das, was uns gefällt*', Wittgenstein said that 'even that is a kind of ethics. It is helpful in silencing objections to a certain attitude. And it should be considered along with other ethical judgments and discussions, in the anthropological study of ethical discussions which we may have to conduct.'

In the period leading up to the *Investigations* he would try to set down the way he had thought about logic in the *Tractatus*. For example: 'In logic we have a *theory*, and this must be simple and neat, for I want to know that whereby language is language. That all this which we call language has imperfections and slag on it, I agree, but I want to come to know *that* which *has* been adulterated. That whereby I am able to *say something*.' What the *Tractatus* says of 'the real sign' (*das eigentliche Zeichen*) or 'the real proposition' would illustrate this. And there is a similar tendency in what it says of ethics. 'The Ethical', which cannot be expressed, is that whereby I am able to think of good and evil at all, even in the impure and nonsensical expressions I have to use.

In the *Tractatus* he would consider different ways of saying something, in order to find what is essential to its expression. As we can see what the various ways of expressing it have in common, we can see what is arbitrary in each of them and distinguish it from what is necessary. Near the beginning of the *Lecture on Ethics* he says: 'if you look through the row of synonyms which I will put before you, you will, I hope, be able to see the characteristic features which they all have in common and these are the characteristic features of Ethics'.

When he wrote the *Brown Book* he would constantly describe 'different ways of doing it', but he did not call them different ways of saying the same thing. Nor did he think we could reach the heart of the matter by seeing what they all have in common. He did not see them as so many fumbling attempts to say what none of them ever does say perfectly. The variety is important— not in order to fix your gaze on the unadulterated form, but to keep you from looking for it.

When he says there that any given language game or system of human communication is 'complete', he means that you fall into confusion if you try to provide a more ample and more perfect system for what may be said in it. Whatever may be said in your new system, it will not be what was said in the original language game. (Think of the advertisements for formalized languages.) When we study ethical systems other than our own, there is a special temptation to interpret them. We are inclined to think that expressions as they are used in those ethical discussions have some significance which they suggest to *us*—instead of looking at what is done with them there. Wittgenstein mentioned *L'homme est bon* and *La femme est bonne*. 'Consider the temptation to think that this must really mean that the man has a masculine goodness and that the woman has a feminine goodness. There may be a very strong temptation to think this. And yet this is not what the French say. What they really mean is what they really say: "*l'homme est bon*" and "*la femme est bonne*". In considering a different system of ethics there may be a strong temptation to think that what seems to *us* to express the justification of an action must be what really justifies it there, whereas the real reasons are the reasons that are given. These *are* the reasons for or against the action. "Reason" doesn't always mean the same thing; and in ethics we have to keep from assuming that reasons must really be of a different sort from what they are seen to be.'

9

On Continuity: Wittgenstein's Ideas, 1938

The word 'continuity' is used in certain connexions in mathematics. It is also used in a great variety of connexions outside mathematics. And there is a use of the word which may be regarded, at least tentatively, as a third use, not identical either with the use in mathematics or with the use outside mathematics, namely its use in philosophy. The reason for this curious position of the philosophical use may appear later.

Both in mathematics and outside mathematics we use the words 'continuous' and 'continuity' in what we call *sentences*. It may be said that 'the elements of any continuous series form an infinite class which is not denumerable' and again that 'We have every reason to think that there was a continuous motion of the body from this point to that.' And at first sight there might seem to be no very essential difference between the way in which the word is used in the one case and in the other. But expressions like 'the use of a word' or 'the way in which a word is used' may be ambiguous. When one speaks of the use of a word, say of the word 'continuous', one may mean primarily the words with which it is connected and the sort of connexions it has with them in sentences. On the other hand, one may mean what is done with these sentences, how they enter into actual conversations and discussions, the part they play in the activities of the people who do use them. It is clear that the use of a word, in this latter sense of the expression, might be very different in two connexions even though there were little difference in what one might call the external appearance of the sentence in each case.

In order, therefore, to see how the use of the words 'continuous' and 'continuity' in mathematics is related to the use of such words outside mathematics we have to ask first how mathematical sentences or propositions themselves are used and how their use is related to the use of non-mathematical or experiential propositions.

I

At first sight it looks as though the difference between mathematical propositions and non-mathematical (experiential) propositions were mainly in the objects they treat of. It seems as though mathematics treated of timeless objects—geometrical figures or abstract aggregates—while experiential propositions treat of real things whose properties approximate in greater or less degree to those of the ideal objects of mathematics. The application of mathematics may be thought of vaguely as a sort of superposition of mathematical objects on real objects to see how far the properties of the real objects agree with and how far they deviate from the properties of the objects of mathematics. What is here superposed in thought is always something that could never be found in the real world, though it may be regarded as a sort of sublimated shadow of things we find in the real world. When we study physical shapes and areas, for instance—physical circles, ellipses, triangles and so on—we may apply propositions of geometry. But the geometrical propositions treat of *geometrical* circles, ellipses and triangles. And these are objects that we can think of but can never perceive or go about among as we do perceive and go about among real things.

On this view, then, geometry, for instance, is almost a kind of physics of ideal or geometrical objects. It formulates laws about them and describes relations between their properties in a way which seems to be closely analogous to that in which we formulate laws about the properties of real objects. In each case the law is supposed to give an exact statement of the object's properties. But in mathematics we have to discover these properties by pure thought and not by experiment and sense perception.

Now one thing that is worth noting about this sort of view is this. If mathematics does treat of ideal mathematical objects, nevertheless the study of mathematics can teach us next to nothing about what sort of objects these are, or even how to tell one from another. This is particularly clear in connexion with 'geometrical triangles' and 'geometrical circles', for instance. When Euclid says that the angles of an equilateral triangle are equal, and proves it, he says nothing as to what we are to understand by such a proposition as 'this angle is equal to that'. He does not mention any method of finding out whether one angle is equal to another or not. As a matter of fact we know that if we are considering any two angles we might by one method arrive at the result that they are equal and by another method arrive at the result that they are unequal. The words 'equal' and 'unequal' take their meaning from the method of measurement that is being talked about. And unless we know what is to be understood by finding out that one thing is equal to another, just to say that they are equal tells us nothing about them. Suppose, then, that Euclid's proposition is about some sort of ideal triangle. Do we know anything more about what this triangle is like—about what its properties are—when we know that all its angles are equal? And similar questions could obviously be asked in connexion with the proposition that all the radii of a circle are equal. But the general point is one which holds not only of geometrical propositions in which the words 'equal' and 'unequal' occur, but throughout geometry altogether. The geometrical propositions which seem to speak of straight lines, of lines intersecting arcs at points and so on neither presuppose nor say anything about *when* we are to speak of lines (what meaning would it have in geometry to ask, 'But how do you know that what you are talking about is really a line?'), how we are to decide whether a line is straight or not, or what sort of thing we should call 'intersecting an arc at a point'.

One way of putting the matter would be to say that in learning the theorems and proofs of geometry we do not learn any application of the words that appear in them. At first sight this is not obvious, partly because propositions in geometry are in the form of ordinary English sentences which look like any other sentences which we might use in speaking about physical things, for instance. We study these sentences and study certain relations between them. We learn, for instance, that a triangle can't be isosceles if it hasn't the angles at the base equal. And it seems as though we knew how these sentences were used. We imagine a use which we never really make of them; which has never been worked out and has no definite characters at all. We imagine a use of them in describing the properties of geometrical figures, but this use never really comes into play because what we attend to is the connexions between the sentences themselves; we don't employ any method for studying the properties of the supposed figures. We imagine that the propositions of geometry treat of these figures in some way analogous to that in which experiential propositions treat of real things. But the analogy is never worked out. It remains very vaguely imagined. And as far as geometry is concerned, there is no reason why it should be worked out; why it should be worked out in one way or another, or why it should be worked out at all. Because no such application ever plays any part in geometry.

And just as we leave very vague the way in which we imagine geometrical propositions treat of geometrical figures, we leave equally vague what sort of things we imagine these figures to be. It seems as though we could explain to anyone learning geometry the sort of things they are. 'A geometrical straight line is roughly this sort of thing (drawing a line), only of course it has no thickness whatever and is perfectly straight. A geometrical circle is roughly this sort of thing (drawing a circle), only of course the distance from the centre is exactly equal at every point.' It seems as though we knew what sort of thing we should say this of; that we could conceive it quite clearly if we wanted to. But we remain content with such expressions as 'roughly this sort of thing' and 'and so on'. We assume vaguely figures constructed according to definite rules, although there are no such rules. And actually, as far as the study of geometry is concerned, it makes no difference how they are constructed.

We are concerned in geometry with sentences, which seem to be sentences in a language treating of—in a discussion of—triangles, circles and so on. And so long as we remain within geometry, so to speak, we are concerned only with these sentences and their relations to one another. We assume vaguely that these sentences have an application, but this is not what we are looking at at the moment. We do not investigate triangles and circles—ideal or otherwise—and ask whether they have one property or another. We don't predict of any geometrical circle that it will have this property or that. Nor do we alter any geometrical proposition or 'law' or any geometrical system in view of new properties that we have discovered in geometrical objects. When we are doing geometry we are not *using* geometrical propositions for the study of or to convey information about circles and triangles; neither about real circles nor about 'geometrical' ones.

The case is similar with arithmetic. One might at first sight be inclined to say that propositions of arithmetic—for instance elementary expressions of addition and multiplication—treat of the properties of ideal mathematical groups or quantities or units; or perhaps that they describe the properties of pure numbers. But arithmetic says nothing about any method of finding out whether one group is equal to two others or not. We learn from arithmetic, say, that $2 + 3 = 5$ or that $25 \times 25 = 625$. But these propositions make no mention of any method of discovering whether a particular group is equal or unequal to another. So that we should not know what it was that they were saying about mathematical groups, supposing that they did treat of them. When we are dealing with low numbers it seems to be the most natural thing to say that we discover whether one group is equal to another by counting them. But counting might be carried out in all sorts of different ways, even though we used exactly the same expressions in connexion with it as we do now. The correct method of counting might be such that after counting the first ten, say, one has to take something different as 'a further unit' (it might be a pair, say), after twenty something different still, and so on. What one means by 'a group of twenty' or by saying that something is equal to a group of twenty might obviously be very different according to what method of counting—what method of measurement—was employed. And the propositions of arithmetic say nothing about any method of counting. When we deal with very large numbers we don't in fact employ simply the methods that we use for counting small groups, but employ methods that are very much more complicated. And in the case of very large groups it may be more obvious that the question 'How many are there in that group?' takes its meaning from a particular method of counting or measuring; and that if the method of measuring referred to were different the question would have a different meaning. The same applies, of course, to such a question as 'Are there as many in this group as in that?' And since arithmetic does not mention any method of measuring, it does not tell us what would be meant by saying that there were so and so many in any particular group, or that there were as many in one group as in another.

In arithmetic we have to do with sentences which seem to speak of this number and that number and of relations between one number and another. And it seems as though we knew how to use these sentences, partly because we do know how to use sentences which speak of different numbers when we are talking about numbers of cows, numbers of cotton pieces and so on. Thus we may come to imagine that in arithmetic these sentences have a use—that they do speak of numbers—although as a matter of fact this use is never mentioned and never plays any part in arithmetic. When we are talking about cotton pieces we talk about numbers, we know how to tell the difference between one number and another, and know what is meant by asking whether the same number has been shipped as was shipped last month. We do not know anything of this sort when we are setting forth propositions of arithmetic. One might say that when we do arithmetic we don't use the sentences that occur in it to talk about or discuss anything at all.

'But surely', it may be said, 'when we learn arithmetic we do learn something about the numbers that enter into it. We do learn something about 100 when we learn that $100 = 4 \times 25$ or that it is the square of 10. And anyone would say that these propositions state certain properties of 100. Or take even a number like 3. Isn't it one of the properties of 3 that when added to itself it gives 6, and isn't this just what we learn when we learn that $3 + 3 = 6$?'

Certainly we may say that in our arithmetic it is a property of 3 that $3 + 3 = 6$; and so that this proposition states a certain property of 3 in our arithmetic. But this would be a misleading way of speaking if it suggested that we are dealing here with a property which 3 has independently of any proposition in arithmetic; or that it is because of a certain property which 3 has that we say in arithmetic that $3 + 3 = 6$.

Suppose, for instance, that there were in some society an arithmetic which employed the same signs as we do and was in most other respects indistinguishable from our arithmetic, but in which it was wrong to say $3 + 3 = 6$ and was correct to say $3 + 3 = 5$. One may feel inclined to say that of course people might in doing arithmetic say '$3 + 3 = 5$', but then they would not mean by '3' what we mean by it, or they would not mean by '5' or '+' or '=' what we mean by them; for if they did, then they could not say '$3 + 3 = 5$' without contradicting themselves.

But what would show whether a member of this society meant by '3' what we mean by it when he said '$3 + 3 = 5$', and so whether he was contradicting himself or not?

It might be said that what he means by '3' in that proposition depends on what he is thinking—on something which goes on in his mind, some experience he has—when he writes or says it. This seems to be saying that if we knew what his experience was in writing down '3' we should know whether he was contradicting himself by going on to say '3 + 3 = 5'. I don't know exactly what sort of experience would be taken to show that he was contradicting himself in going on in that way. But whatever it might be, I do not understand how *any* experience he might have in writing '3' could be contradicted by his writing 3 + 3 = 5. He might have a particular visual image, for instance, or a particular feeling, and he might feel strongly inclined to write 3 + 3 = 6. But would there be anything self-contradictory in supposing him to have exactly the same image or the same feeling and to feel strongly inclined to write 3 + 3 = 5?

But in any case, if we were to try to explain to anyone what we mean by '3' we should never try to describe to him the experiences we had in writing it; and we could hardly expect to find out what he meant by '3' by asking what experiences he had or what went on in his mind at the moment.

If we did try to explain to him what we meant by '3', we might begin with a sort of ostensive definition. We might point to various objects and say 'Here are 3, these again are 3, now I have 3 in my hand', and so on.

Suppose then that he were to say, 'Ah yes, then we're agreed. That's just what I mean by "3" too.' And suppose he were to go on to say, 'That in fact is just what I mean by "3" when I say that 3 + 3 = 5.' One might be inclined to say that then we can't really have been agreed on the ostensive definition. But why not? We are not agreed, apparently, as to what is the correct sum of 3 + 3. But has anything been said about this in the ostensive definition anyway?

It would, of course, be possible for someone to misunderstand an ostensive definition which we gave, and probably it happens fairly often. This is partly because if we define an expression by pointing to something, it is always possible for someone to misunderstand the pointing. If we were to try to explain what we meant by '3' by pointing to a group of 3 stones and saying 'Here are 3', and then someone were to change their arrangement or perhaps to paint them green and ask 'And what are they now?' we should say he had not understood what we meant. (Although here 'what we meant' was not anything that happened at the time we said the words, but is to be found by seeing, for instance, what sorts of questions are considered relevant, what would be taken to show that our statement no longer holds, and so on.) We might say that he did not understand how we were using the words and how we were using pointing in this particular situation.

On the other hand even if there is no misunderstanding of the ostensive definition itself—even if someone understands the pointing and the use of the words in that particular situation—there are still varieties of ways in which he might use this expression in other connexions. Perhaps this is especially obvious if what we are explaining is not the meaning of some substantive but the grammatical function of some expression. Suppose one were trying to explain to someone how we use 'not', and began by giving what we might call an ostensive definition of 'not'. We might do this by first showing him something and then removing it ('not there'), by holding him back from something he was about to do and saying 'not that', or other means. And we might soon find that he understood perfectly how we were using 'not'—what 'not' means in these particular situations. But suppose then that he came upon, or himself felt inclined to use, a double negative. Would anything in the sort of ostensive definition we have given show conclusively how we use a double negation? It may be that many people would be inclined to say that a double negation is grammatically equivalent to an affirmation (though many also would not); but this is not something that has been settled by the explanation we have given of the use of a single 'not'. And there would be nothing *inconsistent* with such an explanation if one didn't admit that two 'not's make an affirmative.

Here again someone might say that it depends on whether we are using 'not' with the same meaning here as we do in the sentence with the single 'not'. Take the sentences 'I have not any' and 'I have not not any'. If 'not' in the second sentence means what it does in the first, it may be said, then obviously the second 'not' removes the negation, and we are left with an affirmation.

But exactly what would 'meaning the same in the second sentence' consist in? This is just what the explanation of the 'not' in the first sentence leaves undecided. By accepting that definition we have not committed ourselves one way or another concerning the use in the second sentence.

(If a man says 'I haven't got any', and a minute later, in order to repeat what he has just said, 'I haven't got none', does he use 'haven't got' in the same sense or in a different sense in the two sentences?)

The case is similar with 3. The ostensive definition may explain its use in certain connexions. But it does not settle all the details of its use in other connexions.

(If in our ostensive definition we pointed to things like stones, chairs and pencils, most people would no doubt say that if you add 3 to 3 the result is 6. This is partly because of the sort of things that stones and chairs are: because if you bring one group of three stones together with another group of three stones, and then count what is there, you almost always find that there are six. If these physical objects behaved differently, if one or more stones suddenly vanished whenever we brought a group of three near to another group of three, we might be inclined to say something different. But one could imagine even less dreamlike circumstances in which one might give the same ostensive definition of three as we should now give, and yet say that when three is added to three there are five. It might be that in most cases when we brought two groups of three objects together, there were two objects in the centre which were either adjoining one another or overlapping; and that we always counted these as one. This might be such an obvious and natural thing to do, and be so much taken for granted, that anyone who had given the ostensive definition of '3' that we have would feel most strongly inclined to say that if 3 is added to 3 the result is 5.)

One might, of course, explain the meaning of '3' not by means of an ostensive definition, but by some such statement as '3 = 1+1+1'. But this would still not settle whether 3+3 = 5, or not. I mean there might still be an arithmetic in which 3+3 = 5. And since the statement that 3 = 1+1+1 says nothing about the result of 3+3, there is not so far any evidence of a contradiction.

'But would you then define "5" by 1+1+1+1+1+1? If so, then you mean by "5" what we mean by "6", and the difference is only a verbal one.'

But I need not define '5' in that way. I might define '5' as it would be defined in ordinary arithmetic; perhaps as $1+1+1+1$ $+1$. And in my arithmetic it might still be correct to say $3+3 = 5$, even though I defined 3 as $1+1+1$.

What, after all, is explained by such a definition as $3 = 1+1+1$? The explanation is enlightening only if you have some idea of what to do with it, of how to make use of it in other connexions. And anyone who gives you the explanation assumes that you *will* have some idea. But the explanation itself doesn't say anything about any use to be made of it. And if I make a different use of it from you, I have not contradicted anything that has been stated in the explanation.

'What we assume in arithmetic, of course, is that you know certain elementary rules of addition. If you do, and if you follow these rules, then, given that $3 = 1+1+1$, there can be only one result of $3+3$, namely 6.'

But is there only one possible way of following these rules? In our arithmetic there is only one way, of course; and if anyone does anything else we say that he is not following the elementary rules of arithmetic. If anyone said $3 = 1+1+1$ and $3+3 = 5$ we should say he did not know how to use the rules of addition. But this is not something that is stated either in the definition of 3, or in an explanation we might give of the rules of addition. We might explain these rules by reference to certain examples, and say 'You always add in that way.' We cannot specify what 'adding in that way' would be in every connexion the pupil will meet; and of course there is no need to do so. But what I am suggesting is that we can imagine a community in which circumstances—special conditions in which arithmetic was applied, perhaps, or combinations of ancient customs—inclined people to say that if you do add in that way, then the result of adding 3 to 3 is 5. They might say that if you said anything else you would not be following the elementary rules of addition.

I suppose someone might say that $3+3$ can't equal 5, just because part of what we mean by '3' is that when it is added to itself the result is 6; because this would be included in any statement of what we mean by '3'.

If we do say this, then of course there is no sense in saying that it is *because* of what we mean by '3' that $3+3 = 6$.

To say that it would be included in any statement of what we mean by '3' comes to saying that you could not explain to anyone how we calculate with 3 unless you explained that $3+3 = 6$. This may be so. But there is no sense in saying that *because* we calculate in this way with 3, we *have* to calculate in this way, or that there would be something unthinkable about calculating in any other way.

The arithmetic of 3—the propositions involving 3 which we say are correct arithmetic—is not contained in or determined by 'what we mean by 3'—as though the arithmetic sprang out of the meaning of '3' like shoots from a bulb. It is less misleading to say that the meaning of 3 is contained in or is given in the whole arithmetic of it. (And if the arithmetic can always be further developed, so can the 'meaning'.) If any part of this arithmetic had been different, then we may say that the meaning would have been different. These two sentences are synonymous. Only when you put it in this way it doesn't seem difficult to imagine that the arithmetic might have been different.

On the other hand, if someone says 'Surely if you mean by the signs what we mean by them, then our arithmetic is the only *possible* one', he is saying something which, in one sense anyway, is perfectly true. It says no more then that what we mean by them is given in our arithmetic of them. But this way of putting it may incline one to go on to say something like, 'The meaning which the signs in our arithmetic have puts the thought of any different arithmetic out of court.'

It is this way of speaking which helps one to think that if $3+3 = 5$ were part of any arithmetic, then either these signs would be used to mean what some proposition in our arithmetic means (say $3+3 = 6$ or $3+2 = 5$) or the proposition would be self-contradictory.

No technique for using an expression can contradict the meaning of that expression, because the meaning is in the technique. A different set of arithmetical propositions involving some numeral could not contradict the meaning of that numeral. They would form a different calculus of it. But no calculus or no arithmetic of a particular numeral either follows from or contradicts the meaning of it. One description of the use of an expression may contradict another description of its use. And one statement as to what is correct arithmetic may contradict another statement as to what is correct arithmetic (taking 'correct arithmetic' to mean what it ordinarily does mean). Thus there can be contradictory statements as to whether $3+3 = 5$ or not. But we do not decide whether $3+3 = 5$ by asking first what '3' means in that proposition.

'But if there is nothing in the nature of numbers which makes the propositions and procedures of arithmetic necessary,' it may be said, 'then it looks as though it were a mere accident that our arithmetic is what it is; as though it might just as well have been quite different, or as though various propositions scattered throughout it might just as well have been different, and that it just happens to be what it is. The whole thing seems to have no more rationality about it than a set of rules of etiquette. And if it were really like that it is hard to see how there could be mathematical problems or mathematical research or mathematical discoveries.'

There could be no mathematical investigation if there were nothing by which our procedure was guided in one way rather than another, and nothing by which our results could be checked to see whether they were right or wrong. If anyone makes a discovery in arithmetic he can give reasons in support of it, convincing to anyone who knows arithmetic; and he can give reasons showing that anything else would be wrong. But this does not mean that the character of arithmetic and the way in which it develops is determined by the properties of numbers.

In the investigation of any arithmetical problem we are guided by certain rules: the rules of arithmetic which, as we say, tell us how to calculate and how to check our calculations. With regard to these rules there are at least two questions I might mention.

(a) Is there only one sort of guidance which our rules of arithmetic could give? What settles the correct way of following the rules? (Not another set of mathematical rules; that would only push the question further back. So is it an appeal to the nature of numbers, or to intuition?)

(b) Are the rules themselves arbitrary, a kind of irrational custom?

I mentioned something connected with the first question when discussing the different uses that may be made of definitions. We explain the meaning of the rules of arithmetic—we teach people how to add and divide, for instance—by stating them and giving certain examples of their use. And we expect people to see from these examples how to use the rules in other connexions. You simply follow the same procedure. We expect people to see what 'following the same procedure' is (perhaps after we have corrected their own efforts in one or two cases), and generally they do. That is, they generally do go on adding and dividing correctly, or if they do not they will admit their mistakes when their attention has been called to them. But we have not *said* what we mean by 'the same procedure' in every connexion. And we can imagine that a person should in certain cases regularly add and divide in a way that we call incorrect, and yet say that he was adding and dividing in the same way that we had shown him, and in the way in which the rules declared correct. For instance we might have shown someone what we mean by 'adding one' to a number, and we might be satisfied that he had understood. He might proceed just as we do for all numbers up to 100; and then he might go on: 102, 104, 106, 108. If we were to protest: 'But you were doing it correctly before; why don't you go on in the same way?' he might reply in all sincerity: 'But surely I *am* going on in the same way.' Well, is he going on in the way in which we taught him, or isn't he?

One might say that what he is doing now shows that he did not understand the explanation we gave. But suppose we gave no explanation of 'adding one' for numbers over 100, beyond the statement that you go on in the same way. We may say that what we meant, although we didn't say it, was that you go on here 101, 102, 103. But this cannot mean that that was part of the explanation we gave, or that there was anything about the explanation we gave which excluded the interpretation of 'going on in the same way' which he took. To say that that is what we meant amounts to saying that that is what we should unhesitatingly have called 'going on in the same way' ourselves if anyone had asked us. That is what we call following the explanation given. But someone might give the same explanation and not agree with us as to what 'following that explanation' would be for numbers over 100. It might be difficult or it might be impossible to teach such a person arithmetic, just because he did not follow explanations of the use of rules in the way in which practically all of us do when we learn arithmetic. But he might still call what he was doing following the rules we use, and say that it was because of these rules that he went on like this. And there would be nothing self-contradictory about his procedure.

We say that we are guided by the rules, and we appeal to the rules of arithmetic in support of our procedure. But there is nothing in these rules which makes a different procedure unthinkable, or which says that you could not proceed differently and still be following these rules. Only this is the way we do arithmetic; this is the way we are taught and teach others. And if you appeal to the rules in support of some other procedure, you still have not shown that what you are doing is correct arithmetic, as we understand that phrase. This doesn't mean that we might just as well not have any rules at all. For most people who have been taught arithmetic do go on correctly when they are told to apply the rule in the same way in a new case. And there are various reasons why this is the most natural thing to do.

It might be suggested that we have a guarantee of the correctness of our procedure, and that this lies in pure intuition, or in a direct apprehension of the nature of numbers. On this view it is an intuition which shows us that it is the same operation of 'adding one' if we go on '101, 102, 103', and that it is not the same operation if we go on '102, 104, 106'. And it may be said generally that it is intuition which shows us which procedures are possible and which are impossible in mathematics.

Here there is a possible unclarity about the phrase 'it is intuition which shows us this'. This might mean that when we take one procedure to be correct and another to be incorrect, we always 'follow our intuition'. This would not show that what we call the correct procedure had any special necessity about it; and there would be no apparent reason why we should not do mathematics correctly without following any intuition, although, on this view, we do not actually do so. On the other hand it may mean that we *know* by intuition that this procedure is correct, and perhaps also that any other procedure is impossible. Not only does the intuition convince us that this way of doing it is correct, but if it is pure intuition which convinces us, then it *is* correct.

But to say 'then it *is* correct' suggests that there is some other criterion of its correctness besides having an intuition of it. And again it seems as though one ought to be able to do mathematics correctly even if no one ever had a pure intuition. In fact he could do mathematics correctly if he were taught in the way in which most of us have been taught. We are given certain rules of addition, subtraction, multiplication, division; we are made to do quantities of exercises, and our mistakes are corrected again and again. Then if we are interested we go on doing mathematics: we go on doing things with the technique we have learned. We are familiar with the distinction between correct and incorrect calculations first of all because we have been told in quantities of cases that what we have done is incorrect and have been shown the correct way. What we are shown in the first instance is a certain procedure—a certain series of sentences —and we are *told* that that is correct, and that what we have written down is incorrect.

Later, of course, a new procedure may strike us as obviously correct mathematics for all sorts of other reasons, such as, for instance, certain striking similarities and analogies with established mathematical procedures, and the fact that the new developments seem to 'fit in with' already existing mathematics in many different ways. I may have more to say in this connexion later. But it is worth noting here that one of the fundamental things guiding anyone in a new development is his knowledge of mathematics; and that this is a knowledge which comes to him originally not from intuition at all, but from training.

'But you have just said that this training does not settle how you will go on in new circumstances.'

I have said there is nothing about a mathematical rule itself, and nothing about the explanation of a mathematical procedure, which settles how it is to be followed (what we are to call 'following it') in all circumstances. But there is a way of doing arithmetic—and so of following the rules—which those who teach us arithmetic call correct, and there are other ways which they call incorrect. And when we have been taught arithmetic we ourselves come to call one way of going on correct and other ways incorrect, even though we may not have been specially taught what to do in these particular cases. That is what happens. And the fact is that we do not need any intuition in order to do this. If some people have an experience which they call 'having an intuition' whenever they work out the answer to a mathematical problem, this is irrelevant. What is relevant is that they have been taught and that they then go on in this way; or they may go on in some other way, and then they have made a mistake in arithmetic.

Of course when someone points out to me a mistake I have made in giving an answer to a problem in arithmetic he does not do so by telling me that those who teach mathematics would say something different. He expects me to see my mistake when he has called my attention to certain things I have done, and perhaps reminded me of what I know to be correct calculations in other connexions. He may be very concerned that I should see the mistake myself, and not simply take his word for it. And there are various things that may make him satisfied that I have done so; it may be simply the question whether when I have admitted that I have made a mistake I can provide the correction to it myself; it may be the question whether when the circumstances are altered slightly I can avoid making a similar sort of mistake; it may be whether I can pick out similar mistakes in answers that are prepared for me. Supposing I can do all these things, he may be satisfied that I have seen what my mistake was. It is very unlikely that he will ever ask whether I had any experience of 'insight' or 'intuition'. He might not be convinced that I had seen my mistake if I told him I had had such an experience. And if he were, he would soon change his mind if he found that I were unable to do any of the other things just mentioned. The point is that when he tries to get me to 'see the mistake myself', it is irrelevant to his purpose whether I have any experience that I should be inclined to call 'intuition' or 'insight'. The distinction which we normally draw between cases in which someone 'sees a mistake in arithmetic himself' and cases in which he merely 'takes another person's word for it' is not a distinction between cases in which someone has an intuition and admits his mistake and cases where someone admits his mistake without having an intuition.

We need no intuition, then, in order to be able to go on correctly in arithmetic, or to distinguish between correct arithmetic and incorrect.

This is connected with the question whether it is unthinkable that correct arithmetic should be different from what we now call correct arithmetic. (Of whether 'although such an arithmetic might be *called* correct, it couldn't really *be* correct'.) The view that the correctness of arithmetic depends on or has its 'source' in intuition suggests that no matter what circumstances might incline us to do arithmetic differently, nevertheless our intuition would show us that such an arithmetic was inherently impossible. I have argued already that there is no reason to call a different arithmetic 'impossible' in the sense of 'self-contradictory'. And this might be admitted by those who hold that arithmetic depends on intuition. (They might insist that you have to distinguish between 'mathematical impossibility' and 'logical impossibility', even though both are *a priori*.) But if we admit that whether a piece of arithmetic is correct or not does not consist in or depend on its being 'given in intuition' (whatever that may mean), then the suggestion that our intuition would show us that a different arithmetic was inherently impossible is not very interesting. I suppose that to say that it was 'inherently impossible' would mean that it could not be given in intuition, or that what was given in intuition would be incompatible with it in some way. But however this might be understood, it has no bearing on the question whether a different arithmetic could be correct.

'Well, is it just a matter of custom, then? Is knowing arithmetic simply a matter of knowing "what's done"? You lay emphasis on the fact that we are taught to do mathematics in this way, and that we teach others to do it in the same way. But is there no *justification* for our teaching people to do mathematics in this way—beyond the fact that that's the way that everybody does it? Is it a matter of sheer accident that people *do* happen to do mathematics in this way? Are you really saying that there is nothing about the nature of mathematics which gives any reason why it should have developed in this form rather than in another?'

I should be willing to say that there is some reason in the nature of mathematics for its developing in the form it has; although I should think that way of speaking unfortunate if it led people to believe that something in the signs and rules we use in mathematics—the 'nature of numbers' or 'intuition of what is the correct way to calculate'—made it unthinkable that mathematics should be done in any other way. There are, I should say, *various* reasons in the nature of mathematics for our doing it in the way we do, although none of these shows that there is any inherent *necessity* for doing it in this way. (The notion of mathematical necessity comes from elsewhere.) Suppose we look on mathematics as a sort of instrument (which is what we do when we apply it). If anyone asked what the nature of some instrument was, I suppose this would be equivalent to asking how it is used or what you do with it. And to say there are reasons in the nature of the instrument for its having this form rather than another would mean that you can see a reason why it has this form if you think of what you are supposed to do with it. Similarly, we can see reasons why we calculate as we do if we consider the sort of application mathematics has.

In a similar way reasons for using one system of measurement and one method of measuring rather than another could be found in 'what we do with' our measurements: what sort of things we measure and what we measure for. If I want to find out whether I can fit certain pieces of furniture into a room, I want rigid instruments to measure with. I want a foot rule that remains the same when I measure the bed and when I measure the wall; if I can place the foot rule ten times 'on end' along the wall, I know I can fit the bed in there all right. But suppose I knew that what I was going to try to fit in somewhere would change its shape when moved about, or would expand greatly when brought into the room, I might try to find some instrument that was not rigid but expanded and contracted in the same way, so that I could know at once by applying the instrument whether what I had measured would go in there or not. And then of course one might want a different way of computing and expressing measurements as well.

I say there might be a *reason* for adopting some different method of measurement in this case because under such circumstances a different method of measurement might be much more *convenient* for the purposes in hand. Given those circumstances, it would be natural for people to do that. This does not mean, of course, that if they didn't do that they would not be measuring at all. The same holds about saying that there is a reason for measuring in the various ways we do now. People might measure in ways that we should regard as very much less convenient and perhaps stupid; perhaps simply because a very long time ago it had been convenient to measure in that way for certain purposes which people then had, and now it is continued for the sake of 'keeping up the old traditions'; or perhaps because people find going through that sort of operation pleasing in itself. If certain ways of measuring were universally adopted, the life of the community might be one which would give us a curious impression of madness. Eddie Cantor, in his film *Strike me Pink*, measures cloth with an elastic yardstick, using the extended yardstick when he is taking the cloth off the roll and when he is asking the customer: 'Is that enough?' and using the shrunken yardstick when he cuts the cloth. It might be a universal practice to have elastic yardsticks, and further each person might pride himself on having his own special degree of elasticity in the yardstick he used. Business in such a community would be rather different from business in ours. But it might go on, and people might, if you asked them, give reasons for preferring it that way.

What I want to emphasize is that when we say that there is a justification or a reason for our measuring in the way we do, this does not mean that there could be no justification for measuring in any other way.

And similarly with mathematics. I say there are reasons for our calculating as we do, and that it is not just a matter of blindly following a custom, without any reason for preferring this custom to any other. But this does not mean that if mathematics were done quite differently there could be no justification for it whatever. There might be nothing which we should regard as a justification for doing mathematics in that way (nothing could persuade us to do it that way), and we might regard it as a stupid waste of time and effort to calculate like that. But there the matter rests. The people in the community where they did calculate like that might shrug their shoulders and say we lacked finer sensibilities, and go on doing mathematics like that. And there would be no 'internal impossibility' about their mathematics.

Those who try to base mathematics on intuition or on the natures of the (von Gott geschaffenen) natural numbers seem to find it unbearable that the matter should rest there, and want to find for mathematics some sort of 'absolute' justification. They want a justification which shows that there could be no justification for anything else. But actually 'intuition' is no help in this. It is no more true that there is only one possible way of 'following your intuition' or 'being guided by intuition' than it is that there is only one possible way of being guided by a mathematical rule. So that even if all persons who do mathematics have intuitions which are perfectly clear, there are still various ways in which mathematics might be done, and in each case it might be claimed that that way was taken because one wanted to follow one's intuition. We could imagine various interpretations which people might give to an intuition, even though such interpretations might seem to us very strange indeed. It is no help to say that we have an intuition of how to interpret our intuition. So that *if* intuition justifies any way of calculating, and if the only justification for calculating in some way is intuition, it still does not follow that there *could* be no justification for calculating in a different way.

There are various circumstances connected with the application of mathematics which provide reasons for our calculating as we do. One of these is the nature and behaviour of the things we generally apply it to. I have referred to this already in connexion with '$3+3 = 6$'. If we count stones or chairs or cows in the way in which a bank clerk counts coins, taking one away at a time, there is nothing which inclines anyone to count two objects as one. If certain of the objects disappeared in the process of counting, or ran together, we might count differently. We are inclined to say $3+3 = 6$ partly because when we bring one group of three stones or chairs together with another group of three stones or chairs, they practically always remain where they are while we count them, and we can count six objects before us. If these objects had behaved very differently while we were bringing them together and counting them, the arithmetic developed for reckoning about them might have been different.

The point here is that although, as I have said, there is nothing about arithmetic which allows of only one sort of application, we are generally much more strongly inclined to apply our elementary arithmetic in one way rather than in any other. And the same holds of Euclidean geometry. There is one way which seems the most simple and direct way of applying any proposition of elementary arithmetic. But we could not apply these propositions in this way, or at any rate the procedure would no longer be so simple, if the things we applied them to generally behaved entirely differently. If one object always vanished when two groups of three were brought together, then '$3+3 = 6$' would not have such an obvious application in predicting what would happen in such a case, and in checking to see how nearly our prediction had been fulfilled. The application would have to be more indirect, and we should probably need auxiliary operations as well as simple counting. And if the same thing or something similar held pretty generally, then our elementary arithmetic as we do it would seem a perverse and cumbersome sort of arithmetic to use.

Similarly, Euclidean geometry grew up in connexion with a particular sort of application. And if the things to which geometry was generally applied had behaved quite differently—if nothing ever held its shape while it was being measured, for instance, or if measurements never showed that two three-sided surfaces having two sides and the included angle equal were anywhere near equal in area—Euclidean geometry would probably not have developed in just the form it did. It would have been an impracticable sort of geometry to use for elementary applications. Its sentences and its passages from one sentence to another would have no obvious connexion with our ordinary ways of speaking about physical things. As it is, the propositions and proofs about triangles and circles and the rest in Euclid do have some connexion with—some resemblance to—what we say in making measurements of physical things, and they fit in naturally to a way of speaking about these measurements. If they did not, we could not use them in just the way we do in connexion with making our measurements more accurate.

Another reason for our calculating as we do lies in what can be easily written down, or written down in a convenient form, with paper and ink. If we had not been able to state our calculations in a convenient symbolism, that could be easily written down and manipulated on paper, certain developments of mathematics might have been different—calculations might have followed different sorts of rules.

Another reason for calculating in one way rather than another has been connected with a wish to systematize mathematics, or some department of mathematics, in a way that is as little cumbersome as possible. There is often a practical justification for this, connected with application. Mathematics has been applied mainly in physics, and physics has been closely connected with engineering. So that the interest of applying mathematics has very often been to make predictions accurate. In this connexion calculations have often to be based on great varieties of measurements and laws. And it is obviously desirable to have a technique by which one can reach one's conclusion, we might say with a minimum of 'bother'. So that certain ways of calculating may have been preferred simply because a different way would have been difficult to fit in with other calculations, and would have made the whole system much more cumbersome.

This wish to avoid complications and bother in a system may influence the sort of things we say in mathematics in various ways. Consider for instance the statement that a tangent to a circle has one and only one point in common with the circumference. Anything that we should call *drawing* a line tangent to a curve would make them have a stretch in common. But if we were to say in geometry that a tangent and a curve have a stretch in common, we should give ourselves no end of trouble in our geometry. There would be questions as to how long or how short such a stretch must be; there would be difficulties as to how we should describe the distinction between a straight line and a curve; and so on. These difficulties are avoided if we say that the tangent and the curve have only a point in common (even though we don't know what would be meant by finding out that this was so) and that nothing we ever draw is quite a geometrical tangent.

Or suppose that we have drawn an ellipse. Suppose then that we find the foci, draw an axis through the foci, and draw a line cutting the ellipse parallel to the big axis. Suppose we then measure at each end of the ellipse the distance between the point where this line cuts the ellipse and the big axis, and suppose the results of our measurements are not quite equal. Should we then say that in some ellipses these distances are unequal? Or should we say that our measurements have been incorrect? If we say the former, it will make enormous trouble in building up a system. And this trouble is avoided if we say that in all ellipses the distances are equal, but measurements may always show deviation in one direction or another.

This is connected with another point. When we apply mathematics it is like describing a situation by reference to some norm. In using mathematics we apply a standard of accuracy to the statements we make in our empirical descriptions. Consider what an application of the proposition of Pythagoras would consist in, for instance. One might draw or mark out somehow a triangle which looked, at any rate, like a right-angled one. One might then measure the sides, calculate the square of the measurements, and see whether the equation held with these measurements. If it did not, then we might conclude either that there had been a mistake in our calculation, or that the measurements were not accurate, or else that what we had drawn was not really a right-angled triangle, although it came pretty near to being one. Or take an application of the proposition that $100/4 = 25$. If I buy a piece of cloth which I believe to be 100 yards long, and after selling 24 pieces from it of 4 yards each I find I have only $3\frac{1}{2}$ yards left, I conclude either that my measurements have been inaccurate, or that the piece was short of 100 yards in the first place.

Here someone might be confused by the suggestion that we apply the proposition of Pythagoras 'to find out whether what we have before us is a right angle or not'. For this might suggest that we were trying to find out something in the sense in which we might if we were trying to find out whether a lump of white material was ivory or not. But we do not conclude from our measurements that what we are examining has or has not some property over and above what we have observed in making the measurements. And in this sense we might say that we do not find out anything.

This is connected with the fact that we do not make experiments to see whether the proposition holds here or not; we *calculate*.

We might say that we 'find out' whether the equation holds with these measurements; which is not like finding out whether an empirical law holds in some case.

This points, then, to a difference between the sense in which we apply a mathematical proposition and the sense in which we apply an empirical law. Just as the purpose of applying it is different.

What we calculate for is not to discover some property of the thing, but to see whether, since it yields these measurements, it is 'really right angled'. To see whether, in calling it right angled, one is speaking quite accurately; or how near to accuracy one comes.

This is the central question; not as to whether one may have made a mistake of fact, but as to whether one is using the words accurately or not.

It is important to recognize that this language about 'exactly equal' and 'exactly a right angle'—or 'a geometrically perfect right angle'—is all part of the description of what we are measuring here; and that it gets its meaning from the part it plays in this description. When we say that this is not a perfect right angle but comes pretty near to being one, we are as it were comparing what we actually have here with what we might have —with some ideal state of affairs. But this comparison enters in only as a way of speaking. No such ideal state of affairs is ever studied, and no comparison is ever drawn in fact between it and what we have before us. The reference to an ideal state of affairs is part of the *phraseology* in which we describe physical angles as 'more nearly', 'not quite' and so on. It is part of the grammar of that way of speaking about physical triangles which we happen to have adopted. And it has no meaning except in connexion with that way of speaking about physical triangles.

There may be various reasons for describing things by reference to a 'norm' or 'ideal of exactitude' in this way. I have said that it may have immense advantages in connexion with prediction. From the point of view of being able to bring what we measure into a system, of being able to see what sort of considerations are relevant or affected by these measurements, it is an advantage to express measurements in terms of agreement with or deviation from an 'ideal case' or 'norm'. It enables one to treat and compare various measurements so to speak under one head. It allows quick and easy comparisons which would otherwise be impossible.

The ideal of exactitude, then, is *an ideal of exactitude in the statements we make*. 'If you want your statement to be perfectly exact, then you mustn't say that the two are equal unless . . .'; and here the rules of calculation come in. And this view of mathematics as setting forth rules of how we are to speak if our statements are to be perfectly exact, is connected with a view of mathematics as presenting us with paradigms—paradigms of reasoning. Mathematics states what is the correct conclusion to draw *if you are being perfectly accurate*. 'But if this is really an isosceles triangle, then those two angles at the base must be *exactly* equal.' It presents us with paradigms of the passage from one step to another; a model of the correct way to proceed. This is probably partly what people have in mind when they say that mathematics is really logic.

But because mathematics presents us with paradigms of reasoning, it looks rather—when we are not engaged in the application of it—as though it presented us with reasonings about paradigms; paradigms of triangles, circles, aggregates and so on—mathematical entities. It is, we might say, a *picture* of reasoning about objects—which however is not an actual reasoning about or drawing conclusions about objects at all. It is what we 'go by' when we do reason about objects. But we don't reason about objects when we do mathematics (apart from any application of it).

'Well, if you say that mathematics sets forth a grammar or a phraseology, and that the study of mathematics is not a study of any objects, is what you are saying that mathematical propositions are propositions about signs?'

What I am saying is that we have given in mathematics a certain way of using signs; that the propositions of mathematics exhibit a certain technique of handling signs. That is what mathematics provides us with. Does it follow that in doing mathematics we *say* anything about these signs?

Mathematics is of course a very much more complicated system (or a set of such systems) than anything that we generally call 'grammar', or than anything we should generally call a phraseology. One might say, 'If it is a phraseology it is certainly an extremely complicated one; and it seems abstruse and far removed from our ordinary language.' But this does not really weaken the analogy between the study and development of mathematics and the study and development of a phraseology or a grammar. For we might answer that mathematics has been developed for speaking about very abstruse and complicated things and happenings, which are not discussed in ordinary conversation. It has been developed for speaking about what is observed under the highly specialized conditions of a laboratory experiment, for instance; for describing the elaborate and complicated ways of measuring that are practised there. Or for describing the elaborate sorts of measurements and predictions that are carried out in an astronomical observatory. It is a phraseology for use in describing very intricate and abstruse observations and in connexion with very intricate and abstruse practices.

I have said that mathematics seems to speak about ideal objects so long as we are not applying it. That is what our mathematical statements are like—they have the form of sentences in which we talk about things. And we may go on thinking of them more or less vaguely as having to do with a realm of ideal objects as long as we are doing mathematics.

But every expression that is used in mathematics can be used in the same sense outside mathematics—i.e., in connexion with the application of mathematics. And expressions which seem, so long as we keep within mathematics itself, to refer to ideal objects, have an application in which a reference to ideal objects has no place at all. In mathematics we may say that we are using such words as 'triangle' and 'ellipse' in the geometrical sense; and since this seems to be a different sense from that in which we speak of a physical triangle or a physical ellipse, it seems as though we were speaking of a different kind of ellipse— namely a geometrical one, which is not found among physical things and cannot be perceived by the senses. But when we measure a physical ellipse we may say that our measurements show that it is not quite a perfect ellipse, or that it deviates slightly from a geometrical ellipse in this or that respect. Here we use the term 'ellipse' in the geometrical sense—in the same sense as it is used in geometry. But nothing in the shape of an ideal object is introduced or plays any part in our measurement of the physical ellipse. If we look at what we do, we try to make our measurements as accurate as possible, to reduce variations and so on; and we see how the results stand in relation to a geometrical formula. No reference is made to any supersensible object. We have used the expression 'geometrical ellipse', and we have used it in the sense in which it is used in geometry; but its function is not to refer to anything in an ideal realm.

There are certain expressions which appear in mathematics of which one might say not that in mathematics they have a different sense from that which they have in a physical statement, but that they have no counterparts in physical or experiential statements at all. Take, for instance, such expressions as 'infinite straight line', or 'infinite series', or 'continuous series'. It might seem that these expressions are used in mathematics to refer to objects which could not possibly be experienced, but which can only be contemplated in pure thought. They may seem to refer to objects which transcend all possible experience, and which are rather overwhelming. But here again if we look at the application that is made of these expressions we find simply that we are using a piece of mathematics, a notation for describing something, and that we have not wandered into a realm that transcends experience at all.

Consider the expression 'infinite straight line', for instance. There might be various reasons for introducing this expression into geometry. What we first call straight lines are stretches which begin somewhere and end somewhere. We may then have the idea of stretches added to one another, and of a line which includes not only this stretch but other stretches beyond it. We may then come to speak of 'going on in the same straight line' beyond any stretch we may take. We may then come to form the idea or picture of a line from which any length, no matter how great, may be taken. This picture may correspond in a way to a certain impression. Consider the impression we get from looking along a short bit of wire, for instance, as contrasted with that which we might get from looking along a piece of wire that was so long that we could not see the end of it. That is a particular impression among others. And it may help us to form the picture of a line which we call an 'infinite straight line' which differs from finite straight lines or stretches rather in the way in which the impression of the wire of which we can't see the end differs from the impression of the bit of wire of which we can see the end.

Now there may be advantages in speaking of 'an infinite straight line' when we want to speak about 'going on in the same straight line' without meaning 'going on within this finite stretch'. But then they can only be the advantages of one phrase over another, and can have nothing to do with recognizing differences between one kind of line and another. When we speak of a body continuing in motion in the same straight line, or when we say of three stars that they lie in the same straight line, it is nonsense to ask where this line begins or when it ends. When we say that a body is still moving in the same straight line, we are not using 'straight line' in such a way that it would have any sense to ask when it will come to the end of the line, or to speak of stopping before it got to the end. We use the phrase 'a straight line' in such connexions, and we use it differently from the way in which we use it when we are speaking of a particular stretch. But we have not introduced any ideal object called 'an infinite straight line'. We have introduced nothing that is ideal and nothing that is an object. We have introduced a way of speaking in the description of these phenomena. We have here, if you like, an application of the phrase 'a straight line without end'. But in this application the picture of something huge, that goes beyond everything that we could possibly experience, becomes useless and rather ridiculous.

(It may be instructive here to compare the use of such a phrase as 'an infinite supply of money'. Suppose you have commissioned me to do some piece of work, and tell me I have only to ask you for any money I want in connexion with it. I might ask, 'Well, up to what sum? There is a limit I suppose.' And you might reply, 'No, there's none. There is an infinite supply, and you can draw any sum you like. None is too great.' Here one might form the picture of 'an infinite supply', which is a supply like any other—only infinite. Whereas the phrase 'infinite supply of money' is not supposed in this connexion to distinguish or describe a particular supply—a particular sum—at all. If it were, it would be contrary to your purposes. For if it were a particular sum, and you told me I could take any sum, then I might take that, and there would be no more. Whereas what you wanted to tell me was that there would always be more.)

Similarly in connexion with such a phrase as 'infinite series', 'continuous series', 'continuum', we may form a picture which at first seems rather overwhelming, but which has little relation to the way in which the phrase is actually used.

We may use the picture of 'the number continuum' or 'the number line', for instance. We think of a line, and of the natural numbers arranged along it somehow, say from left to right. We then say that between any two natural numbers there are rationals, and that between any two rationals there is another rational; and that there is no end to this.

This is already a rather overpowering picture, and seems to go beyond anything that we are familiar with in the physical world when we speak of a series of things with other things between them. But then we go on to say that there are still *gaps* in this series of rationals—and further that these are gaps that can be filled by *points*. We say that in these gaps between rationals there are irrationals, transcendental numbers, and so on, in greater profusion than the series of rationals itself.

Such a picture might itself be a strong inducement to say that we are concerned here with a line or series that can only be studied in pure thought, and never in the physical world.

Consider what it comes to when we actually make use of the expressions that have led to the construction of this picture.

Take for instance the reference to 'gaps' in the series of rational numbers (or 'rational points'), and to irrational numbers as being 'in' or as 'filling' these gaps. Take for instance the statement that π lies between two rationals. What this comes to in application is that if you measure the circumference of a circle and say it is $d\pi$, then every *rational* measure will be inexact; will be either too much or too little.

But most of the mathematics of the continuum has no such direct application to physical things.

I have said that the reasons for the way in which mathematics has developed are mainly connected with the application of it. I have said, for instance, that it is an advantage from the point of view of predictions to have different calculations systematized in a form as little cumbersome as possible. And my discussion suggested that the main interest in developing and perfecting mathematical systems was a practical one—an interest in making mathematics more convenient for applications. In a certain sense I think perhaps we may say that this practical interest has been the fundamental one that has led to the development of mathematical systems—in the sense that without it the work of systematizing mathematics would never have been begun. But there is also another interest in the development of mathematics, which might be called aesthetic. This may appear when people are concerned to achieve greater 'elegance' in some mathematical system, for instance; or in certain efforts to obtain greater simplicity, greater uniformity between different deductions, and so on. And this sort of interest may lead to an elaboration of mathematics, and the development of new branches of mathematics without reference to any possible application at all. It leads to the construction of what we might call systems of 'empty connexions'. It may be that applications of these new branches of mathematics will be found, perhaps quite shortly, perhaps only after many years; that has happened, of course. Or it may be that no application will ever be found. Again, if some new branch of mathematics is given an application, this may be in some rather unexpected way.

For instance, it may be that an application is found for some new branch of mathematics, but not an application directly to physical phenomena at all, but rather to the process of doing mathematics itself. It may turn out to be extremely useful in giving an account of certain mathematical procedures.

In some ways it is like certain things one might imagine people to do in connexion with map-making. Suppose there were a map of England showing various railway lines. Suppose some of these lines meet in junctions, and others, although they are not parallel, do not meet, but run to the coast without, so to speak, ever coming to the apex of the angle. Someone might then wish to draw a map of England in which the lines which do not meet in England are extended so as to meet at points in the ocean, or on the continent or elsewhere. If someone were then to use this map, there would be part of it that could be directly applied, although for our ordinary present purposes it would be over-complicated and cumbersome; and until we had become familiar with it, it might be misleading. But someone might want this map not for any use that it could be put to, but for some aesthetic reason. It might seem intolerably untidy—full of yawning gaps—to have lines on a map which just stop without meeting. Again, some parts of the elaboration may prove directly applicable at some later date—for instance if huge bridges or tunnels are built leading to points which are here shown as junctions on the map.

On the other hand it may turn out that what we have con-structed, the elaborations that have been made—turns out to be very useful for some other purpose, not for the ordinary pur-pose of a map at all. It might be that the points thus marked on the map as 'junctions in the ocean' turned out to be very useful as centres from which to turn a compass in doing certain things in the continuation of the rest of the map. They might, in other words, prove very useful as applied—applied in an entirely different way—to the process of map-making.

The continuum in mathematics is a *composition*—in the sense in which we talk of a composition in music. I don't mean that it is a work of free fantasy. In composing the continuum mathe-maticians are guided. But they are here guided not so much by the nature of physical things as by the nature of already existing mathematics—they are guided, that is, by analogies with other departments of mathematics, by the notion of 'going on', and other things.

If one were to use the language of the mathematics of the continuum in describing physical things, it would in the majority of cases be a hopelessly cumbersone way of speaking. If I were to describe this paving stone as a continuum of points, and try to use the mathematical language for a continuous series of three dimensions, this way of speaking would, for almost every imaginable purpose, be nothing but a hindrance. It would be a way of speaking that provides for and would apparently lead to all sorts of statements for which we could imagine no use whatever.

The same holds if one were to apply the mathematical language about a 'continuous series of points'. This way of speaking, for instance, provides for a distinction between such a scrics and a series that consists only of rational points. But in connexion with physical things we should have to say that we could not tell the difference—and do not know what would be meant by telling the difference—between a continuous series and a series which leaves out the irrational points, say. And if that is so, why introduce this way of speaking at all?

This holds generally about speaking of 'infinite series', different types of infinite series, and so on. These expressions, and the mathematics connected with them, have no use as applied directly to physical things.

But if one obeys the order, 'Write down an infinite series' or 'Write down an infinite series of such-and-such properties', one is applying the word; and the mathematics of it is used in the description of what it is that one is then writing down, of what one is doing.

Similarly, if we use the mathematics of the continuum to describe procedures in the theory of functions, for example, we are giving it an application in which it is not a cumbersome way of speaking but a highly convenient one.

Mathematical statements are applied in different ways.

In certain cases there seems to be a fairly close parallel between the way in which we use 'continuous' in mathematics and the way in which we use 'continuous' outside mathematics; in other cases not.

Consider methods of persuading someone that a curve is a continuous aggregate of points. We have determined the curve when we have determined the positions of points lying in it. So all that really matters is positions of points. If we alter the positions of points, we alter the nature of the curve. Well then, you have already got the curve when you have got the positions of points determining it. Only, of course, it must be *all* the points. —We might put this by saying: 'It is really just an aggregate of points in such and such positions (which can be specified), only it must be a *continuous* aggregate.'

Suppose we were to give an equation: $y = f(x)$. We draw the curve of this equation. And we might say then, 'You see, you have the whole thing when you have relations between numbers.'—Or take $y = x^2$. We might then say, 'You see what this equation is. If you put certain numbers in one column (the y column) you have certain others corresponding to them in another column (the x^2 column). So what the equation amounts to is just a table of numbers arranged in a certain way.'

What one does here is to imagine a sort of hypothetical table: one which never is and never could be written down. (What you write down is: 'something like this . . . . *and so on*'.) You say the equation is this hypothetical table—and you then go on working with the equation.

The case is similar when we say the line is really an aggregate of points. We can specify an actual aggregate of points lying in the curve. And we say that the whole curve is really just such an aggregate taken 'and so on'—and then we go on working with the curve.

When they speak about the procedure of determining a curve, for example, some mathematicians seem inclined to place one part of the procedure in the foreground and push another part into the background. A curve is drawn with coordinates. What is pushed to the fore is: the axes, the lines drawn to points on the curve, and so on. What is left more in the background is the whole process of calculating y when you know x; the whole technique of using the graph.—We have a mirage of an imaginary table of values, which could not exist, and which would not replace the equation if it did.

If a mathematician says 'a curve is made up of points', we may ask 'Which points?' If he replies 'All the points', then we do not know what is meant by this unless he shows us the technique of *finding* all the points. Otherwise it tells us nothing. How does he go through this technique? (Does he end by drawing the line?)

I have said 'he goes on working with the curve'. Where the curve comes into this calculation he may say he is concerned with a continuous function or continuous series. And he may speak of points in the curve in expressing his calculations. In all this he is constructing a concept 'curve of such and such properties'. But such a proposition as 'the curve is made up of points' will never enter. For his calculations it will make no difference whether he says this or not. It he says 'the curve is a continuous aggregate of points', he is not telling us how curves are made up. He is saying something about certain calculations which he calls calculations with curves. He is telling us something about a paradigm. This is a paradigm for the use of the term, or for the use of calculations, in certain applications in physics, or in applications to other parts of mathematics. He is working out or constructing a grammar, a phraseology.

'Does mathematics tell us about the nature of continuity?'— If we say it does, what is meant is that propositions of mathematics are about a paradigm of continuity. And this might be said, perhaps.

II

There would be no point in using the word 'continuity' in mathematics unless it were meant to have some connexion with its uses outside mathematics. And in fact we talk in mathematics about a continuous curve, we use the adjective 'continuous' in connexion with 'lines', 'surfaces' and so on— expressions with which we use it also outside mathematics.

But if there is a proposition in mathematics that such and such a curve is continuous, then in mathematics this is either postulated or *proved*. Outside mathematics, in experience, we never prove that something is continuous; although we may have ways of finding out whether it is or not. Whereas in mathematics we never find out that something is continuous.— This shows that a different sort of thing is being said. If we say that propositions of mathematics assert that something is continuous at all, this is an entirely different sort of assertion from that made in non-mathematical statements.

I want to speak of the notion of 'continuity' outside mathematics under three main heads, although I cannot keep them quite separate:

(1) 'Continuity' as applied to sense data; chiefly: visual continuity.

(2) Finding out whether something is continuous in physics.

(3) A puzzling feature of continuity: the inclination to think that continuity must really be a form of discontinuity. This is

connected with (a) a mode of setting things down on paper—a portrayal which must be discontinuous; and (b) a confusion of the visual with the physical sense of 'continuous', so that what seems continuous really is not, and perhaps what we call continuous is ultimately a special form of discontinuity. This produces a puzzle which makes us want to dig deeper into what we are dealing with. (It seems as though we wanted a microscope— but we do not. What we want is to know the connexions of the thing—not what it would look like if we saw clearly.)

I

We may speak of subjective continuity, or of the continuity or discontinuity of sense data. I may say that the red surface looks continuous to me, or that the flashing lights on the sign give me an impression of a continuous movement; and I may go on to speak of the continuity of the impression.

Not that the 'subjective' application is always the same. We may speak of a sense datum as a continuous expanse of colour, or a continuous strip, as opposed to a series of dashes. What is essential for the continuity of the impression here is, roughly, that there should be no gaps in it.—On the other hand, we may speak of the continuous change in a sense datum. And this may be a change over a period of time, such as the changing shape of a visual figure, or a continuously changing colour or temperature or pitch. Or it may be a variation that is spread out and simultaneous, as in a continuously shaded surface.—When I speak of continuous variation in the sense datum, this is a different application of the word from: 'it is a continuous expanse'. I'd say the variation was discontinuous now, if it were broken or abrupt; I should not mean that it was 'discrete' or 'intermittent'. Roughly, what is essential for the continuity of a variation is that it should not be sudden. A 'break in the continuity' of a variation is not like a break in the continuity of a strip or a sound.

If I call a sense datum or impression continuous, then obviously there can be no investigation to see whether it really is so. But neither is it like speaking of a continuous transformation in mathematics.

'It looks continuous, but *is* it really?' would have no sense if we were speaking of the visual impression throughout. And yet we may be led to ask whether visual curves are really continuous. Are visual curves made up of straight bits?

If someone did say 'every visual curve is composed of straight bits', how should we understand this? It might be merely a matter of terminology. At the outset, anyway, we do not know what sort of thing he is calling a curve and what he is calling straight bits.

And we might ask, 'as opposed to what? What would be a curve that was *not* made up of straight bits?'—There are various answers he might give.

He may tell us he sees a circle made up of straight bits, and that when he says a certain bit is straight he means to contrast it with a line which curves ∩ or ⋏, or some such.—Or he might say it had straight bits only when it was a ring made up of alternating black and white squares.*

Suppose we cannot distinguish a visual circle from a visual 100-sided regular polygon. We might still say it was a continuous curve, to distinguish it from something like a pentagon which we *can* distinguish easily from a curve.

In other words, we can give a use to the sentence 'This curve is composed of straight bits, and that curve is not composed of straight bits.' And we may be inclined to say that some visual curves are composed of straight bits, without meaning by this that they are discontinuous curves. Even if we said '*all* visual curves are composed of straight bits' we could still distinguish between those that are not continuous and those that are. And the objection that 'they aren't *really* continuous' may mean only that we are not using the word here as we do in mathematics—which of course is true.—The point is that if we call certain visual curves continuous we are not making any mistake about facts.

'Is the visual field continuous?'—We should be inclined to say it is. And this looks like a perfectly good English sentence. But except for the fact that we'd be inclined to answer in this way, it is not a sentence for which we have any use.—We never ask when the visual field is continuous and when it is not. And I should have no definite notion of anything from which I was distinguishing 'my visual field' by saying that it is continuous.

* Cf. Wittgenstein's illustration, *Remarks on the Foundations of Mathematics*, I, §§96, 97.

In certain circumstances a man might say there were gaps in his visual field. If there were a black spot which always remained perfectly stationary, and everything moved not 'behind' it but around it . . . we might be inclined to refer to this as a gap.—But it may not be like that, and we may not know at all how he is using the word when he says there are gaps. Even if he points to a hole and says 'This is what I see'—I may still not know. Partly because I see that too, and I am not inclined to say there are gaps in my visual field: I do not know why he should call that a gap rather than something else a gap,—etc.

So we cannot say that just because we are inclined to say that the visual field is continuous we should know what anyone meant if he said it wasn't.

So long as we keep to the impression or appearance, there can be no question of finding out whether it is continuous or not. But it is important that we should not forget or neglect the ways in which we may speak of subjective continuity—the compatibilities and incompatibilities that go with 'looks continuous' or 'looks discontinuous', for instance,— because, for one thing, our (subjective) impressions of continuity and of discontinuity may influence the notation in which we do describe or investigate the continuity of physical things and processes; and because of the constant tendency to confuse visual continuity with physical continuity—leading us to contrast what the body's movement *seems* to be with what it 'really is', and so perhaps to ask whether everything that is taken to be continuous may not be really discontinuous after all.

These confusions are fostered by the 'objectification' in the phraseology of 'sense data': I may say either 'the movement looks continuous to me' or 'I have a sense datum which *is* continuous'. These are simply alternative ways of speaking. But the sense datum phraseology suggests that there is something— some *object*—which is continuous, and which might be set over against the physical object (the physical motion) and compared with it.—And then why should we not ask what the sense datum 'really is', just as we ask this about physical things? This would be a crazy thing to ask. It would mean we were treating the form or schema of the physical investigation as though it could be applied without any reference to the circumstances in which it may have sense. This is what people have done in connexion with the idea of *minima visibilia*, for instance.

How do we find a minimum visible? We could give a surface divided into black and white squares, then take it with each square sub-divided, and so on. When the whole surface looks grey, we have passed the minimum visible black or white square. And we may experiment to find the last distinct impression. But we have to emphasize that here what is a *minimum* that can be seen is not the minimum *object* that can be seen, not the minimum impression that we had. We *can* call it the minimum impression, if we mean: the minimum impression that can be produced by this means—as opposed to giving him alcohol.

There is also a totally different thing which we might call the smallest possible visual impression. 'The shapeless dot.' And then we may ask: does my visual impression of a blue sky consist of shapeless dots?—The answer would be: If you mean, 'Do I see shapeless dots?', no. If you say it *must* consist of them, this comes to replacing the expression 'continuous blue area of the visual field' by 'continuous aggregate of blue shapeless dots'. Here I am using the essentially discontinuous picture of 'aggregate', qualifying it for my purposes by the adjective 'continuous'. This is a change of names, not of facts.

2

(i) Suppose someone asks whether this physical object is really continuous. There are various criteria, various methods, we might use to decide this. (To begin with, we might use a magnifying glass; or, if we are asking whether a movement is continuous, we might take a 'slow-motion' picture of it; and we may go on to more refined methods.) But even then, there may be considerations which suggest that 'still, they are not *really* continuous'.

One such influence may lie in the pictures which (for most of us) seem to sum up our use of a word like 'continuous' or 'discontinuous'; or again, pictures which sum up and partly determine our use of a word like 'thing' or 'collection' (or 'aggregate'). And there may be a 'prelingual' activity of deciding whether to say that a chair, for example, is like • or is like •••••. Whether it is like a ball or a collection of balls. When I talk about the chair I may be inclined to identify it first with one sort of picture and then with the other. 'But obviously it has separate constituents: it's *this*.'—'But surely it is one thing: it's *this*.' If this uncertainty persists, we may come to think that we hardly ever have to do with what is really one single thing. This comes partly from repeated disappointments: after thinking that the one picture • fits, we find that the other (.•.•.) fits after all. Perhaps we come then to think that nothing is a single thing except an atom or a proton.—The picture of atomic structure (from chemistry and physics) would be an influence as well. We may want to say that everything is really a collection of atoms.

If we then feel inclined to use the word 'continuous' only where we would speak of a single thing (where there is no sort of separation), we may be inclined to say that no physical surface is really continuous.

If we do, this is not connected with any investigation. 'Is any physical surface really continuous?' is not a question in physics —or in practical affairs.

We might have the phrase 'a surface that's perfectly smooth'. We can describe ways of making a surface smoother and smoother. Or, if we are trying to determine whether it *is* smooth or not, we can point to what has been done to make the investigation more and more accurate, and consider how we could make it more accurate still. We can then say that perfect smoothness can never be reached, and still speak of our procedure as approximating to an ideal of smoothness. (Instead of 'smoothness of the surface' we could have put 'continuity of the surface'.)

This is a matter of adopting a phraseology. The description by reference to an ideal is simply a kind or form of description. It is not that I show anyone an ideal and say that the surface is more or less like this.

It is a phraseology, or way of speaking, that might be suggested by the trend of investigations, as we refine our methods further and further, or make the measurements more and more accurate. We could speak in the same sense of an *investigation* which is only an ideal, to which tests and experiments approximate.

If in physics there are reasons which lead us to say that no way of smoothing the surface can lead to real continuity, or that tests could never show that it was really continuous, we may still use an idea of perfect continuity—use a certain picture —in describing the facts. Or physicists may speak of a *maximum* of continuity, or minimum of discontinuity. They may then rule out the expression 'perfect continuity'; or they may not. They may describe the facts both in terms of a maximum and (in other circumstances) in terms of an ideal.

It is obvious that to say in such connexions 'Perfect continuity can never be reached' or 'We never have a surface that is perfectly continuous' is not a statement about what things are like. It is not a theory or hypothesis which might be tested.

(If we speak of an ideal of accuracy in weighing, should we say that 'nothing ever has a weight, but only plus or minus'— in contrast with the way things *might* have been?)

'Was the body moving continuously when it went from A to B?' is not the sort of question we would ask in ordinary life. And the best way to see what it means is to see what we would look for to decide it. In this case the natural method would be: to find whether it left out anything, any position, whether there were any 'jumps' in its passage from A to B.

We might take various means of discovering gaps. We might take a cinematograph picture at very great speed ('slow motion') and in certain cases this might show us gaps which we could not notice otherwise. Or we might place wires for electric signals very close together all along the line on which the body would move. It might be that one of these would not register, and this would show that the motion had been discontinuous.

But it may be said that this method has a limit beyond which it could not be used: the wires themselves have a certain thickness, or the time interval between the body's contact with the one and its contact with the other is too short to be recorded, or something of the sort. (Here we have something like a quantum.) It makes no sense to try to determine by this method whether anything is left out below a certain interval.—There may be a calculation in physics which will demonstrate that it is impossible to tell whether, within an interval smaller than such and such a minimum, motion was continuous or not.

Well, then, shall we say you cannot decide—that it is inherently impossible ('impossible in principle') that we should ever decide whether the motion was continuous or not?—This is not obvious.

We could say all motion is discontinuous: however it moves, there must at least be a jump of such and such an interval.

On the other hand, we might speak here of approximating

to an ideal of continuity. In physics there may be a quantum or limit beyond which it is senseless to speak of *continuing* this approximation to an ideal of continuity. But this does nothing to discredit the ideal or rob it of meaning.

Suppose one said that beyond 1/100,000 of a millimetre it has no sense to speak of making physical measurements of a diameter with a measuring rod more accurate, because that is the diameter of an atom. Therefore we could never determine whether the circumference of a circle was really π times the diameter. But would the fact that we can never get beyond a certain point in making our measurements more accurate do anything to discredit π? π in fact shows us what would be meant by making measurements more accurate. And this remains.—If someone said that the quantum did show that π was something 'mythical', he would be deceived by the same misunderstanding which leads one to ask, 'Where do you get this ideal, then?' It is the assumption that we are imagining something to which something else approximates; and that 'if you can't treat it experimentally, there is no meaning in saying that there is any such thing'. But we had not said 'there is any such thing' in the sense which he is assuming.

Return now to our difficulty about 'leaves out anything'. We can construct a method to find out. But we must emphasize that we do not know in advance what we are trying to find out, and it is this method itself which gives a meaning to the phrase.— We might have taken other ways of finding out, and then the phrase would have had different senses. For instance: (1) Suppose the motion occurred entirely within my visual field, and I looked carefully to see if it jumped or not. No, it didn't—and that settles it. If I had no impression of its jumping, then there is (in this method) no further question. Or (2) Suppose the motion was not one which I could survey entirely myself, and I stationed men at various intervals along the path: each man is to observe a stretch which he can himself survey, and this is a stretch between two others.—These are different games, and the statement 'It didn't leave out anything' has a different verification in each case.

If someone says that we would never call it a serious attempt to find out unless we used instruments and measures—all right. But then he is fixing the sense of 'leave out anything'.

Consider, 'It moved over all positions except one.' It may

seem that if it has sense to say 'it didn't move over this point', it must have sense to say 'it didn't move over this point but it moved over every other.' But here we may have a use of 'all' in which 'all except one' has no meaning; although English grammar allows for it.

We can speak of 'all points of the surface'—the surface is painted red all over: every point is red. But we do not know how we should set out to verify 'all points of the surface except one are painted red.'

(The point of asking what the verification is in a case of this sort is just to keep one from being deceived by the form of the English sentence.)

We can say, 'The two lines have all their points either below or above one another except the point at which they intersect.' And if someone said, 'Its motion covered all positions in the path except this one'—it may seem as though we could build up a method to verify this. We may say that what you have to do is to see whether it goes past a certain point. We may define a set of points to be investigated: first we take the point midway in the path, then the quarters, the eighths and so on. We might then, with some sort of ideal compass, construct $\sqrt{2}$ and check that point.—But the trouble here is that we do not know how this 'see whether it goes by a certain point' is to be applied. Is it to be: a certain point plus or minus? How are we to know whether it goes by *just this point*? We do not know what would count as an application of this—until we know what the technique actually is.

(I said earlier that we do have methods to see whether it left out this or that point. But not 'methods to see whether it left out *only* this point'.)

What misleads us here is that 'see whether it goes past a certain point' seems familiar, as indeed it is. But then we go on with an imaginary method of 'investigating (checking) points' —as though this phrase meant something even if we cannot think of any application of it.

(ii) I want to pass from: investigating to see whether some physical object or process is continuous or not, to: *theories* of continuity.

Everything that one might call a theory of continuity, or of continuous motion, tries to explain continuity by a form of discontinuity. But there are two very different things which this might mean.

1. We could imagine a theory in physics to explain what we now call continuous motion: explaining the phenomenon by reference to discontinuous processes.

2. We may want to give an explanation of continuity (or of continuous motion) in quite a different sense, and to say that all continuity is a *form* of discontinuity. This might apply also to the visual continuity of visual motion. In any case, it would be applied in a different way from an explanation in physics.

The physical theory might be something more or less analogous to this: Imagine that events on a cinema screen were being observed and investigated by people who did not know their causes. The investigation leads them to find the projector and the film and the rest; and they find that what they originally supposed to be moving shadows of moving bodies is in fact a rapid succession of discrete stationary shadows. And it might be said: We can imagine that in some analogous way what appears to be the movement of a body in three-dimensional space is really some sort of three-dimensional screen play. But here we must distinguish different roles which such a theory might have —differences in what we'd mean by speaking of a theory:

(a) Experiments may have shown us the existence of some discontinuous phenomena which we can suitably describe by saying that discrete pictures of a body are projected into three-dimensional space. This may be a working hypothesis of physics, borne out by experiments, but something we do not try to extend beyond these special cases.

(b) It may be something a physicist says, simply because it sounds sensational. He may compare God to a cinema operator who projects history onto a three-dimensional screen. In this case, what in (a) was a working hypothesis may be simply a pleasing picture which no one tries to verify or refute.

(c) Suppose that in certain special cases the theory has been firmly established by experiment: a theory explaining what we had always thought was continuous motion in terms of some discontinuous process. We may then want to unify our picture of reality and say that *all* motion is really discontinuous.

'Perhaps some time it will be shown that all continuity is really discontinuity.' The puzzling words are 'perhaps *it will be shown*'. What sort of experiment would this be? What would incline anyone to make such a general statement? In a particular case we may look through a magnifying glass and see something discontinuous. And we may say then since it looks discontinuous under a magnifying glass it really is discontinuous. This is connected with all sorts of things about the magnifying glass and the way we use it. All this *inclines* us to say it is really discontinuous —although we are not compelled to say this, in the sense in which we are compelled to say we *see* something discontinuous when we look through a magnifying glass at it.

In any case, we'd never say this showed that *all* continuity was really discontinuous. We should have no idea of the sort of experiment that might make us want to say that.

If physicists said it had been shown by physical science that all motion was discontinuous, this might mean either:

(1) that physics had discovered something like quantum which showed it was *impossible* for a body to move more than such-and-such a very small distance without vanishing and then (generally) reappearing after a 'jump'; or

(2) that a great many motions or sorts of motions, when viewed under conditions of these and these experiments, had been seen to be discontinuous, and probably this would be found to be the case with all motions.

But whichever of these be meant, it would not show that we must change anything in our former way of speaking. We could still distinguish between continuous and discontinuous motion as we always have.—It might be, of course, that we'd feel we did want to change our way of speaking—that we preferred now to speak only of 'different degrees of discontinuity'. There might be certain practical advantages in this. And we might prefer to have a unified terminology: 'If in connexion with those experiments you say the motion is discontinuous, you ought to use this term for it always.' But why need you? May there not be circumstances—those which led you to make the distinction in the first place—in which it would be an advantage *not* to have just this unification?

We are inclined to say that the experiment showed that continuous motion is not what we thought it was. But did we think about what would happen in the special conditions of this experiment at all?

'Well, if in spite of the new discoveries you do still speak of "continuous motion" in such-and-such cases, you are using the expression in an *inexact* sense now, since motion has been shown to be really discontinuous.'—But *must* we say that what seemed continuous is really discontinuous?—The expressions 'seems' and 'really is' are what confuse us here.

At the bottom of all our notation, our way of thinking in these matters, is the distinction between visual continuity and physical discontinuity. The words 'continuous' and 'discontinuous' are connected first and foremost each with a particular picture. This is continuous: ⌒ ; this is discontinuous: . . . . It is not at all clear a priori that we must describe some phenomenon as *really* being . . . . , although appearing to be ⌒ ; and not rather as *being* ⌒ although *connected* in a particular way with a discontinuous process.

What theory we adopt will depend on practical considerations: which one enables us to predict events in the simplest way. But it will also depend on considerations which we might in a *very loose* way call aesthetic. We could call it 'continuous though connected in a particular way with a discontinuous process', even in the case where it appears discontinuous under a magnifying glass. But it might be a highly— stupidly—inconvenient sort of theory which did this. On the other hand, suppose we take a photograph of a star on a moving film and instead of getting a smudge we get discrete images. Certain circumstances might make the idea that a star emits discontinuous light almost intolerable, and we would explain the results by the character of the film. Or we may be forced to admit that it *is* a discontinuous emission of light and cannot be explained by the film.

We may be inclined to explain apparent discontinuity by continuity—saying that the appearance of discontinuity is 'only' due to so and so. Or we may be inclined to explain away continuous motion at all costs, and to hypostatize a discontinuity behind every continuous appearance.

3

On the other hand, we may want to explain continuity by discontinuity in a different sense altogether—not by giving a physical theory or hypothesis. We may want to say that all continuity is a *form* of discontinuity. In this case we do not hypostatize a discontinuity behind the continuity, but we say that continuity *in its essence* must be a form of discontinuity; as it were, *continuous* discontinuity. (We could also use 'aggregate'.)

Sometimes these two senses of 'explaining continuity' come close together.—Should we say that all motion consists of atoms? This might be said as a theory borne out by the facts, or merely as a way of speaking that we might adopt; by analogy with the atomic theory of matter.—Any very general empirical statement or general law may come to be treated more and more as a norm or way of speaking about phenomena.

If you are asked what motion is, or to give an illustration of it, the most natural thing is to make a movement of the hand. And then nothing is easier than to distinguish motion and positions. There are these and these positions, and the body (the hand) passes through them when it moves. Positions are fixed and discrete, and no one would confuse them with motion. Positions are just what motion is not.

But from the point of view of science we are not inclined to take this subjective continuity (continuity as seen) very seriously. Just as equality of length means to us first and foremost equality established by measurement, whereas equality of length as seen is only a crude anticipation of the real equality—so we think of the seen continuity of movement only as the first incentive to form the real idea of continuity. After all, a movement may look continuous, and it may then be shown that it is not. So we cannot trust our senses. If we want to find out what it really is, we must measure. (Here we forget that one needs one's senses to make measurements.) Perhaps we should say: to be really *justified* in applying the subjective picture of continuous motion to reality, we should have to make a check at every point in the path. ('To make sure none was skipped'—although we have no idea what making such a check would be.)

But to speak so of 'being really justified in applying the picture' would be confused and obscure. We do apply the picture of visual continuity when we look to see whether the body's movement is continuous or not. If we now go on to ask when the application would be really justified, this is because some physical theory ('every process is really discontinuous') has seemed to make its application suspect. But in saying 'for it really to be justified there would have to be . . .' we have not said anything about an application, real or imagined. Perhaps the illusion of measurements makes it look as though we were *pointing* to a case in which it would really be applicable. But no pointing ever takes place. We have made a connexion between the expression 'visually continuous motion' and the expression 'making a check at every point in the path'. But what is gained by this?

The notion of 'applying a picture' of continuous motion—or applying a mode of representing it—would be something like applying a notation. If we 'assign' an object to each of the signs in a notation (or to some group of them), this does not tell us what we do with the notation, or what we'd call an application of it.

We seem to have a conflict between two ways of looking at motion—looking at it as something like the movement of a hand before our eyes, or looking at it as a series of positions. And we look for a way of treating—*developing* almost—the subjective picture of continuous motion that will assimilate it to the idea that motion is all positions. It may seem as though we could do this when we ask: Under what circumstances would this be the right picture of a movement studied by physics?

But now 'the *right* picture' is the phrase that misleads us. I have said that for anyone engaged in science the picture associated with positions and measurements will be the prior one. But we could also give grounds for claiming that the subjective picture (the visual impression) is the prior one. We could argue that unless the phrase 'continuous motion' were connected with *seen* continuous motion in some way, we could not begin to understand the remarks in which those words occurred.—Try to explain to someone what motion is, without assuming that he can see or have any experience of it.—This is one reason why we cannot just *dismiss* the subjective picture of continuity (any more than we disregard our senses when we trust to measurements). But the illusion here is of something like a *perfect coincidence* of visual continuity and physical motion. Almost a sort of congruence. And 'Are we justified in applying it?' means something like: 'Does it *fit*?' Not a question for investigation in physics.

Suppose we ask, 'Does Euclidean geometry fit our space?' Here we generally have a wrong idea of fitting, because we start with a wrong idea of the kind of investigation which would show whether it fits or not. We start with a picture of a more or less refined *optical* investigation—instead of thinking of the mass of widely disparate experiments (electric charges, astronomical investigations ...) which could possibly be called an investigation into whether Euclidean geometry fits our space.

We may think of space as a scaffolding for bodies or matter which occupy it. The scaffolding would then be determined by our geometry, though not, in a sense, described by it—as though space were an ideal object in space. The problem is not whether Euclidean geometry gives a correct description of physical space. It is a question of the applicability of a system of concepts or grammar.

In certain departments—measurements involving very great distances in astronomy, perhaps, where methods and data made it unnatural to try to speak of them in terms of Euclidean lines and angles: it would be a pointless and stupid contrivance if we tried—we could say this is not the geometry that fits. Problems often could not be formulated or decided in terms of it, etc.

If anyone asks, 'Is physical space continuous? does it have all the points the mathematical continuum would allow it to have?'—I suppose this has analogies with 'Does this body's movement include all the points in the path from A to B? does it leave out any point?' If you wish to say the body has passed through $2^{\aleph_0}$ positions, there is so far no objection to this; but nothing in its favour either. Does it help you anywhere?

'Does physical space have such-and-such a multiplicity of points?'—This always looks as though we were asking about some physical volume, like a volume of air, of which we could give the dimensions. As though it were something which has a measurable extension, which might conceivably be different at different times, something which is divisible by these and these methods, and so on. But obviously the question 'What is the extension of physical space?' would be meaningless unless the phrase has a different grammar, and the question a different point, from anything we'd ask about the extension of 'something extended'. Similarly, when we ask about the continuity of a physical surface, we cannot ask in this sense about the continuity of physical space.

Suppose it were said that there is a limit to the possible divisions within any physical measurement of length, since the electron and the proton have effective diameters of 10^{-13} centimetres; so it would be meaningless to speak of differences in length below this magnitude. Perhaps then we should say that a series of points in physical space is a series of possible divisions; or, of points that can be given in terms of physical lengths from a given point. This would not be anything like a series with mathematical continuity.

If we said there are atoms of motion, we should bring in time-atoms too. I do not think anyone does this now. Whitrow refers to it as 'the hypothesis of minimal natural processes and changes, according to which no process can occur in less than some atomic unit of time, the *chronon*', and as the idea of 'successive discrete states between which no other states can be inter-polated. Conversely, in a temporal continuum there would be no successive states, for between any pair we could interpolate intermediate states.'*

As it stands, this is certainly confused. We do not know how one 'state' is divided from another. And it were highly arbitrary to talk of some 'natural' division between time-atoms, or talk of a natural division between space-atoms. There may be a limit to what we call 'trying to determine whether there is a difference in length' or 'trying to determine whether there is a difference in duration'; a limit to what we can ask for, a limit to what we can speak of as verifiable, and so on. But when we say this, we have not introduced anything like a *structure*, atoms *making up* a volume, or making up a process.

'Motion consists entirely of positions' could be compared with 'all motions are circular with deviations'. We could use the expression 'circular with deviations' to describe a rather limited variety of motions: it might be useful in these special cases and the description would serve to distinguish them from motions of other sorts. Then we find that we can extend this notion and call *every* movement circular with deviations. We could even prove this. But then the statement becomes a geometrical one, not a physical one. It is not a *description* of motions at all now, for it tells you nothing about them. It is just a notation or a way of speaking. And the proof would be a geometrical proof.

What does the passage of a body from one place to another consist in? Is it in no place during that passage? or in some places? or in all the places which lie between its start and its finish? Does it in some sense vanish as soon as it starts moving? I mean, does it cease to exist in the sense in which it exists in one place, assume a kind of evanescent state, and reappear only

---

* G. J. Whitrow, *The Natural Philosophy of Time*, London, 1961, p. 153. These are views he refers to, not views he is defending.

when it is once again at rest?—Well, why should we not say this? (You would hardly say it of the motor-car in which you were riding.) If I do say a moving body does not exist while moving, I do not mean it has been destroyed, that we shall never be able to use it again, we had better make another, and so on. I am not trying to give a *theory* of continuous motion.

(Think of the ways in which people have spoken of 'being' and 'becoming', 'process' and 'reality'; of 'potentiality' and 'fulfilment'; of the reality of motion as 'an essentially uncompleted reality', and so on.)

I am confused by conflicting pictures; partly because of what I can represent on paper and what I cannot. It is easy to draw what gives an impression of a body at rest, but not to draw a billiard ball moving. If I draw the path over which it moves, this is not a representation of a motion. I may end by giving a row of 'stills'; or only one, with interpenetrating shadows of the ball on either side of it. (We generally disregard the fact that the ball is rolling, not sliding.) When I ask 'What does its passage from A to B consist in?' I have in mind a picture taken from what we see when a body moves fairly quickly before our eyes. We have a slightly blurred image of it while it is moving and a clear one when it is at rest.

If you ask me whether the billiard ball now moving across the table is in any position while it is moving, I would say yes, since at any rate it is roughly *there* now, and roughly *there* now. And if it is roughly somewhere now, it must be *exactly* somewhere now.—The trouble is that I could have said the same thing, apparently—'it is roughly there now'—if I had been referring to a body at *rest* in this area. And then when I pass from 'it is roughly there' to 'it is *there*' I give it a place which it cannot have and still be moving.—I want to say that the body moving from A to B is in this precise position between A and B and not at rest. So that if I say it is moving there I do not mean what I meant before when I said 'it is moving within these limits or within this space'. I mean something new which is expressed by 'it is passing *through* this position'.

If then someone asks 'through how many positions does it pass between A and B?' the question may baffle me, and in the end I may say 'through all the positions between A and B'. But the sense of 'it is passing through *this* position' was connected with methods of specifying what position it is and checking the time at which it passes through it. And with 'passing through all the positions' this is lost. Ask me to give the positions through which it passes at intervals of 1 second during its motion from A to B, and I know what is meant. But not with 'Give all the positions through which it passes in moving from A to B'— unless this means something which has no similarity to what we normally call 'giving positions of a body during its motion . . .'.

Incidentally, 'through *all* the positions' is not an answer to 'How many?' If someone does ask 'through how many?', it might be because we mention positions when we measure acceleration in a movement, for instance. So the motion includes these positions at least. And to suggest that the motion consists of positions *plus* something else (a kind of mortar between them) seems stupid. So it is not just *those* positions, but the rest is positions also; which seems like saying, 'not just this number, but a whole aggregate of others'.

We could put the question whether continuity of motion is a *form* of discontinuity by asking: 'Is continuous motion one or many?' And this is similar to: 'Is a curve, say a circle, one or does it have parts?' I might say 'First tell me how you are speaking of parts here.' For it might mean what it does when we say that some parts are thick and some are thin, or some parts red and some green, or 'it has parts' could mean just that we can divide it. And yet we are inclined sometimes to answer straight off, without waiting for an explanation—simply because we are so used to calling certain things 'parts of'. We react with 'yes' or 'no', mainly according to our preoccupations —according to the standpoint from which we look at it. This is why we forget that there can be correct and apparently contradictory answers to these questions (questions about the simplicity of circles, for instance, or of motion).

One might say '*Obviously* there are parts to this circle'; or again, 'Obviously this circle is *one*, there's nothing we'd call parts of it.' To the first of these we might ask what the parts of the circle are, and he might point first to certain sectors; if we then asked why just those, since the circle could be divided in other ways (and if there are overlapping parts, then which are the ones that make it up?), he might say finally that it consists of points. For the other answer ('this circle is *one*'), 'There is nothing we call "the parts of the circle" ' would be analogous to 'There is nothing we call "the sides of the circle".' 'Sides' is a special case of 'parts' here.

Neither answer is meant to be an empirical statement. The two parties may agree on all questions of experience. When I say 'There are no parts to a circle', I am not telling you the properties of something we call a 'circle'. The remark, as I mean it, describes my idea in connexion with this word. It describes an image which illustrates the meaning but in a way that, in a sense, *precedes* the use of the word: we are still at the stage of forming the meaning—not applying the word with this meaning; a stage which is *prelingual*. The image may be used as an illustration settling how the word is to be used—as one might make an illustration in notes for a lecture. We *could* use this picture in all sorts of ways. But actually we are inclined to use it in one way rather than others. And giving this illustration settles how we are going to use the word. 'The circle is *one*' is what I might say if I asked myself, 'Now how do I mean that?'

'By "circle" we mean one undivided whole'. 'The circle is a unity shape, namely this: O.' '*Circularity* has no parts.' 'A circle is *this* whole: . . . (whirling so fast you can't see any parts).' 'The circular shape is always undivided.'—In none of these sentences do I *use* the word 'circle'; I am making *preparations* for the use of it.

'The circle is undivided.' Well, and what then? We might say that then we had better not talk about parts of a circle. This would not be exactly a grammatical rule, but in a sense it is laying down a law. So that, for instance, where objects are to be counted we naturally take each circle as one. Or where we describe some complicated design, say 🎯, we would say it was composed of three circles rather than describe it in various other ways; and so on.

I might also have said: 'It is the *essence* of the circular shape that it is one.' Which amounts to: 'This is how we *must* imagine it.'

In the same way we might have answered: 'Clearly a continuous motion consists of parts.' And if someone asked which are the parts of the continuous movement that we're watching we might refer to earlier and later parts; and then to avoid the trouble of overlapping parts we might say it consists of points or positions. Or we might have said, 'Look, it's all *one* movement.'

—It depends on what it is about motion that chiefly interests us.

I have been asking what makes us inclined to say that continuous motion consists of positions of the moving body.—It would be queer to say this if you were watching the movements of a ballet dancer, for instance. But we are inclined to express ourselves in this way when we are preoccupied with places and times. And there is much in our everyday speech that makes it seem natural. I have suggested

(1) That in physics we look for and draw conclusions from the positions of a moving body at particular times.

(2) In our everyday language we can always ask where the moving body is. If we start with 'now it is somewhere *there*', then as we make the 'now' more precise we also narrow down the limits within which we say it is moving. This suggests that for every moment of its motion there is a position.

(3) We are inclined to say that the movement from A to B has parts. We are often ready to speak of parts almost as though the word had an absolute meaning like 'bricks' or 'boards'. The difficulty of overlapping then leads us to assume elements which do not overlap—positions.

(4) We can often give an explanation of what appears to be continuous motion, by showing (or assuming) that the body is in such-and-such discrete positions at discrete times. And, up to a point, the denser (if we use this expression) the series of positions, the closer the resemblance between continuous and discontinuous change of place.—But a thousand-sided regular polygon is no less similar to a circle than is a hundred-thousand-sided polygon. And it would be wrong to say absolutely 'the denser the more similar'. After a point this is not true.

(5) What we put on paper: The picture we make of a line is almost always a dash, the picture of a point is a dot. We are often told we cannot imagine an absolute point or an absolute line. In other words, we think of a point as something extremely small, a line as something extremely thin. If instead of using pencils and pens to draw our figures we used paint brushes, covering a sheet of paper with colours and representing a line by a colour boundary, a point by the intersection of two colour boundaries—many of our ideas and our forms of expression would be entirely different. Nothing would be more ridiculous than to say of a colour boundary that it is thin, or of the intersection that it is extremely small. That a colour boundary could

consist of such intersection points would be a most unhappy word-picture.

All this leads us to develop a phraseology which extends the form: that a body is in certain positions at certain times, into the expression of all that we say about motion. This means we must provide for all the ordinary uses of the word by introducing all sorts of clauses, such as 'passing through all the points be-tween A and B'. And in doing this we often get sentences for which we have no application at all. If a sphere, say a billiard ball, moves in a straight line from A to B, we could, of course, express this by saying that the centre of the sphere passes through all the points on that line (i.e., substitute this expression for 'moves in a straight line from A to B'). But then our phraseology would allow: 'It passed through all the points but one', or 'It passed through all but a thousand of the points', and we have *no* use for these statements. We are using a system of word-pictures, in some ways attractive, in many ways perhaps prac-tical, but allowing of many *redundant* pictures which form so many temptations to forget how our words are actually used.

Think of a phrase like 'complete description' or 'completely described'. We may want to say that the motion of a body can be completely described by giving its position at all times during its motion. But then we have to add that we can never do this; unless we are going to use the phrase 'giving all the positions' for something which has no similarity to what we normally call giving the positions of a body. For of course we may say that the body moves in a circle with the centre so and so and the radius so and so. And if we are going to call this 'giving all the positions of the body', then we *have* given all the positions of the body. But obviously we have only substituted one phrase for another, and we have used an elaborate picture where its elaborateness does not help us to represent the facts.

Similarly, if someone says 'for the purposes of mathematics a line is points', this is a one-sided representation of what mathe-maticians are interested in—a representation that stems from certain modern parts of mathematics, such as the theory of sets. We are easily confused because, for one thing, we are vague about the uses of words like 'can', 'possible', 'impossible'; we say that we cannot count the leaves on the tree within a minute, and also that we cannot write down all the cardinals.—

'We cannot determine whether the body left out one position in the course of its motion.' The consolation that this is due to human frailty would work less well if we had a clearer picture of the game we play with 'human frailty'.

We are tempted to try to build up continuity, and the building stones are to be positions or points. At least it seems as though this is what we are trying to do. We are inclined to say continuity is puzzling: the body which is moving continuously is somewhere and nowhere, or it exists and again doesn't exist. Yet continuous motion is not in the least puzzling ordinarily. We see it about us constantly, and we do not find difficulties in describing it—i.e., doing what we call 'describing the motion of a body'. It begins to be puzzling when we try to speak of it in the phraseology of discontinuity and rest.

When the actual usage of a word resembles, not one game played according to strict rules, but rather an activity approaching sometimes this game, sometimes that, moving irregularly (floating about) between them, then nothing we could call *one* system of rules will describe this usage. We have then to describe various games, giving *various* sets of rules, serving as *centres of variation.*—It is like describing facial characteristics of a population by giving half a dozen photographs of characteristic types.

INDEX

Abbildung, 4
absolute value, 94f.
aggregate, 135, 140, 148, 153
agreement, 56ff.
'all', 26, 38, 85
  'all the points', 135, 150
  '— except one', 144, 156
  'all the positions', 153
analysis, conceptual, 44, 50
  logical, 7, 9, 10, 24
  scientific, 44
Anscombe, G. E. M., 1–16
'anthropological method', 50, 101
applying a picture or notation, 149
arbitrary, 29, 51, 52, 115
arithmetic, 31–6, 107ff.
asking, 80, 85
atomic unit of time, 151

Bedeutungskörper, 17
Black, Max, 23ff.
borderline questions, 87, 89

centres of variation, 157
common understanding, 84
completeness, 51, 52
conceptual analysis, 44, 50
  and psychoanalysis, 45, 46
consensus, 57
constants, logical, 13, 18, 24
continuity, vii, 104ff.
  in sense data, 137f.
  maximum or minimum, 141
  of a physical thing, 140f.
  outside mathematics, 136ff.
  theories of, 144ff.
continuous series, 135
  variation, 137
continuum in mathematics, 133
conversation, 66, 67, 79
  unlike a game, 81
correct arithmetic, 114, 117–20
counting, 108

custom, 100, 115, 120

definition, 58, 61
describing a feeling, 59f.
describing a practice, a rule, 44, 45
describing in terms of an ideal, 141,
  142
discontinuity, 137, 142, 145
  of motion, 146, 147

elementary propositions, 21, 22, 24
equal, 105, 106, 108f.
equations, 23, 31
essence, 154
ethical problems, 98f.
  propositions, 94, 97, 98f.
  systems, 100, 101
exactitude, 43, 44
excluded middle, 90

facts, 11
'family resemblance', 71
following a rule, 55, 66, 113,
  115–18
  the words, 67
form, 32, 34, 74
form of life, 83
formal series, 3, 32–6

'game', 71f.
gaps, 142
  in the visual field, 139
general form of operation, 32–6,
  38, 47
general rule, 4, 5, 22
generality of mathematics, 32
  of the word 'language', 73
'geometrical ellipse', 129
geometrical place, 91
geometry, 105–7, 124
grammatical investigation, 44

having something to say, 81

159